DEFYING THE ODDS

MY STORY

Pauline Thompson

Cover design by Laura Leonard

For my beautiful mum ... my best friend. I love and miss you so much.

For my partner ... I will always love you.

FOREWORD

As an editor of memoirs, I have read many life stories. The details of each person's life are unique. Some people faced abuse and loneliness as children, while others were involved in violent or abusive relationships as adults. Some people encountered discrimination as children, while others were subjected to it in adulthood. Others experienced addiction or physical or mental health issues at certain points in their lives.

However, everyone – and this applies to the whole of the human race – has one thing in common. We all encounter difficulties, struggles and challenges at various stages of our lives. Whether it is a difficult childhood, an unhappy marriage or a sudden bereavement, some events affect us deeply, often at the most unexpected times.

In *Defying the Odds*, Pauline has been extremely honest and open about her struggles. At different times of her life, she has faced abuse, discrimination, health issues and bereavement. Her life has taken many unexpected twists and turns, but she has always been true to herself.

Defying the Odds is based on Pauline's diaries which she has written intermittently since her teenage years. This has allowed her to write about events and recreate conversations from many years ago without relying on her memory entirely. I think writing a diary has also helped her to get to know herself very well and follow her heart.

Even in tough situations, Pauline's humour shines through. She is able to see the lighter side of life, and this has helped her through the difficult times. Pauline's love of music has brought her great joy, even when life has been difficult. Jane McDonald's music is particularly special to her. She has been a fan for over twenty years and has met Jane several times. They share the same Yorkshire roots and a profound love of music.

As well as being a writer, Pauline is also a poet. Her first published book was a collection of poetry entitled *Say What You Feel*.

When Pauline showed me her poem, *Staying Strong*, which she wrote during the COVID-19 pandemic and which was read out on BBC Radio Sheffield in November 2020, I was impressed, especially by the ending. I asked if I could publish it in my online magazine *Small Steps*, which aims to inspire people to move forward in life one step at a time. Pauline agreed. Since then, I have read more of Pauline's poems, and I have been moved by the depths of feeling and compassion for others in her poetry. Pauline has included three of her poems in *Defying the Odds*.

Pauline's story is a story of survival against all the odds, a story of walking away from abusive relationships, a story of being true to yourself no matter what others say or think, a story of finding the love of your life unexpectedly, a story of coping with devastating loss, and a story of living with panic attacks, phobias and health issues.

It is a story of profound joy and intense sadness, of self-doubt and self-discovery.

Pauline's story reminds us to cherish the moments we spend with our loved ones and store them in our hearts, because they can be taken away from us in the blink of an eye. It also reminds us to spend time with and listen to the people in society who may feel left out and ignored by others. They have a story to tell too. We may be surprised by what we hear if we take the time to talk with them and find out more about their lives.

The ups and downs of life, the changes that we go through, the times when we feel like the safety net has been pulled out from underneath us. Through it all, we need to remain strong, as Pauline has, so that we defy the odds.

We all have a unique story to tell, and this is Pauline's story. Let her story inspire you to carry on, no matter what life brings your way.

Roz Andrews

Writer, Editor and Self-Publisher

RA Writers for Hire Ltd

PROLOGUE

'This is the first time we've had the opportunity to be alone this evening.'

'It's been a good evening, though,' I commented.

'Are you okay?'

'I'm fine.'

'Are you sure? Because something is telling me that you're not.'

'I don't want to discuss it at the moment,' I stated.

'I'm always here if you need to talk.'

'I know.'

'I enjoyed the hug we had last time I was here.'

'It was just a hug,' I nervously replied.

'Being so close to you felt good.'

I thought, *God, I'm not prepared for this.* I needed another drink. I went into the kitchen and poured us both a drink and we stood talking.

'How did it make you feel?'

'I'm unsure of my feelings, though it was different to previous hugs,' I admitted.

'There's something I need to tell you.'

'What's that?' I asked.

At that point, the front door opened.

CHAPTER 1

A Stolen Childhood

I often think about how my childhood was ruined by the evil man that was my father. The man who never had any time for me and certainly didn't love me. From an early age, I heard and witnessed a lot of shouting within the home and Mum crying a lot. My father was handy with his fists, especially when he had been drinking. It wasn't until I got older, maybe ten or eleven and into my early teens, that I realised just how bad things were for Mum. He was the type of man who always had to be in control. I was an only child and quite shy, which mainly stemmed from not being allowed to speak up or have an opinion within the family home when my father was around. Often when I opened my mouth to speak, it was frowned upon by him. I would occasionally want to read something I had written at school, but as soon as I opened my exercise book and started reading, my father ordered me to shut up and sit down.

He always used to hit Mum on New Year's Eve. They didn't go out, but he would always drink a bottle of whisky in the house. By the time he had reached the bottom of the bottle, he was in a fighting mood, and

Mum was once again at the receiving end of his fists. One New Year's Eve, when he was hitting Mum, I was so frightened that I ran downstairs, unlocked the front door, and opened it. I was ready to go and get help from one of our neighbours, when the lounge door opened and out came my petrified Mum. I stared in horror as I noticed blood on her face from a cut lip, while my intoxicated father was hovering in the background with blood on his knuckles. She saw me in the hallway and shouted, 'Come on, we're going.' We both flew out of the house and ran down an alleyway across the road. We were able to hide, but still see the house. The cold night air sank into our faces and arms as we stood there in our slippers, shivering.

After a while, we walked to my friend's house, a couple of streets away, to ask if we could borrow coats. They were surprised to see us at the door at that time of night, and shocked to see the blood on Mum's face. They invited us in, made us a hot drink, and were happy for us to borrow coats. My friend's mum suggested that we stayed with them for the night. We declined as Mum had decided that we would go to my grandmother's (my father's mother) who lived just up the road from us. Mum said that it was about time she found out exactly what her son was doing, because this secret had been kept for far too long. So, we stayed with her, and the next morning she came down to our house with us. She intended to give her son a good talking-to.

Luckily, when we arrived, my father was out, which meant we were able to gather a few things together and go back to my grandmother's house. By now, Mum's lip was swollen and bruised, and I hated seeing my beautiful mum looking that way. My father was a wife beater and needed to be locked up, but Mum was so frightened of the repercussions if she reported the incidents to the police, therefore he always got away with it. I often wondered if he would have been as keen to use his fists on a man, someone the same build as him - I somehow think not!

Later that day, we went to stay with my other grandparents - my mum's parents. This wasn't the first time this had happened. Mum left my father on several occasions during my childhood, and we always stayed with her parents. They were a lovely couple, so thoughtful and caring. They were regular church-goers and couldn't tolerate any form of violence. We were usually there for a few weeks and then my father would turn up, full of remorse and empty promises. Mum was always taken in when he persuaded us to go back home. I feel that she always lived in hope and believed that this time things might be different if we went back with him, plus we needed the security of a family home. However, it was always short-lived and a few months later we were back at my grandparents' house.

So, once again, we were staying with my grandparents and I was enjoying being there, but each time we stayed it caused a lot of disruption for me as I had to be allocated to a different school and start looking for new friends. A couple of weeks after we arrived at my grandparents' house, I asked my mum if I could have a dog of my own. I loved dogs and had wanted one for some time. My mum wasn't too keen at first and didn't think that my grandparents would allow me to keep one in their home. However, they agreed, and we got a young dog; I was ecstatic. I was jumping up and down, saying, 'Thank you, thank you!' She was a beautiful, affectionate, jet black puppy with loving eyes, and soft fur. I called her Judy. We used to play ball in the garden, or Mum and I would take her on a long walk.

It was wonderful having my own dog to look after; she was my responsibility, and I did look after her. Weeks went by and eventually my father turned up, once again, asking Mum to go back home. Reluctantly, she agreed on one condition, which was that I could take the dog with me. My father said that was fine - it would be nice to have a pet in the family home. So, back home we went, along with our new dog. Everything seemed fine at first, and it did appear that he had changed. He was being nice to me, the way a father should be with his daughter, and I thought, *Why can't things be like this all the time?*

However, once again it was short-lived. In less than a month, he had returned to his old ways, and he told me to get rid of my dog. I was heartbroken. She was only a mongrel, but she was mine and I loved her. My mum tried to talk my father into letting me keep the dog, but he was having none of it. He had decided that she had to go and that was that. He put the lead on the dog, and shoved her feeding bowl, food, treats, and toys in a carrier bag. He ordered me to take her out and find a new home for her, and not to return home until I had got rid of her. So, I was walking the streets in tears trying to find a new home for my much-loved dog. I knew that I would be in serious trouble if I returned home with her, so I needed to find someone to take her in. As we were walking, I was telling her how much I loved her, and that I would never forget about her. I just wanted to run away with my dog, but I would never have left Mum, plus I knew that I would have been in big trouble if I hadn't returned home.

Luckily, a friend of my auntie adopted her. As she lived only a few doors away from my auntie, it meant that I would still be able to see her when I visited. I was heartbroken because of what he had made me do. *What type of father would inflict such pain and sorrow on his own daughter?* I wondered. He was an animal and I hated him.

As a child, I always enjoyed visiting my grandmother (my father's mother). She used to make me toast on a toasting fork held over the open coal fire. She served it on a floral-patterned plate with creamy butter. It was the best toast ever; you've not had proper toast until you've had it done on a coal fire. She grew up in Lancashire and she would tell me about what life was like for her as a child, and when she got older and used to work in 'service.' This meant that she was a maid in the house of a wealthier family, which was a common form of employment for girls at that time. She used to tell me the same stories each time I visited, but I was more than happy to sit and listen. She loved the fact that I used to visit her on a regular basis. I was happy to do so as I have always been fascinated by the stories that the older generation tell, even as a child. It was a place of refuge, just me, grandma, and the cosy open fire. I felt safe, secure, and loved.

My father worked for the National Coal Board, as it was called at that time, which meant that he was allowed a free delivery of coal several times a year. We had more than enough coal for our needs, so he used to give some to his mother. We had a car in the garage, yet he made Mum and I bag the coal up in to sacks and push it up the road balanced on Mum's bike to deliver it to *his* mother. Of course, we obeyed as we wouldn't have dared not to.

My father always kept Mum short of money, but she still managed to make sure that she gave me a little bit of pocket money each week. She wasn't allowed to have a life outside the home; she couldn't visit friends or go into town shopping on her own. She was even chastised at times for visiting her own parents. However, he was always happy for us to visit his mother, as he could never be bothered to go himself.

He was more than happy for Mum to go to work. There was a method in his madness - he reduced her housekeeping once she was earning her own money. He paid all the household utility bills and gave Mum £10 a week housekeeping. Out of that, she had to buy all the food, my clothes, his tobacco, and other household essential items. She also had to give him money for fuel if she went out anywhere in the car. On the odd occasion that he took Mum out for the evening, she used to have to pay for her own drinks. My father would buy anyone a drink, anyone except Mum. She had to pay for her own. He was the perfect gentleman in public, and no one would ever have guessed he was the bully that he always seemed to turn into once he was at home. As the saying goes, no one knows what goes on behind closed doors.

I despised the way my father treated Mum; she was such a lovely person, and he made her life a misery.

She was a real home maker and always kept our home looking lovely. She was a good cook too - she needed to be, as my father came from a family where good home-cooked meals were always served up, so he came to expect it.

He would often insist on having steak, but I don't think he was giving Mum enough housekeeping to be able to demand steak at mealtimes on a regular basis. However, Mum used to cut back on other things in order to buy steak for him, just to keep the peace. So, he would be sitting at the table with his rump steak, chips, and all the trimmings, while Mum and I would be having something different as we weren't allowed steak. Mum had the job of cooking the steak for him and it had to be perfect. God help Mum if it wasn't cooked to his liking. I have known her get a back-hander if it was slightly over done. We all used to sit at the table, and my father used to look quite pleased with himself because he was eating steak and we had a lesser meal. With each mouthful that he took, I used to think, *I hope it chokes you.*

My father used to go out regularly on his own at the weekend, and my mum and I always made the most of it. We were able to watch what we wanted on TV or play a board game, and Mum always made sure that she had some chocolates for us, or she would make a big bowl of proper homemade chips for us to share. It was lovely spending time with Mum while the bully was out of the way. However, at some point he was to return, and if he had drunk too much, he would be violent. She always knew how much my father had had to drink just by looking at his eyes, and it was the look in those eyes that always determined whether he would be hitting her that night.

I would be lying in bed too frightened to go to sleep in case he came home and started hitting Mum. Shortly after he had returned home, I used to hear raised voices. I would get out of bed and go to the top of the stairs, where I would hear Mum crying and shouting for him to stop as fist hit flesh. I sat there, rigid with fear. I was a child, and I was witnessing what this animal of a man was doing to Mum, and there was nothing I could do about it. This certainly wasn't the way a young child should have to be living. He was around six-foot tall and well built, and Mum was only five-foot, so she never stood a chance against him.

As I entered my early teens, I enjoyed spending time with friends in the evening, but I always had to be back home by 7:30 pm. If I was five minutes late, I was grounded for two or three days. On the occasions when I had been grounded, I used to ask my best friend if she would call round in the evening and try to persuade my father to let me go out, but it never worked. He was having none of it.

This went on right up until I left school and started working. It was frustrating for me as I had friends and cousins who were staying out until around 9 pm having a great time, but I was the one who always had to go running back home to ensure I was in for 7:30 pm. Friends of mine were going to school discos, but initially I wasn't allowed to go. However, Mum managed to talk my father into letting me go on one occasion, which surprised us both. The school disco started around 7:30 pm and finished at 10 pm, and I was told I could go if I was back home by 9:30 pm. To me, it was hardly worth going but I still went as it was nice to be allowed out two hours longer than usual. I remember enjoying the short time that I was there, and I returned home on time. To be honest, I'm surprised I had any friends when I was a child because it was very rare that I could go anywhere with them or do anything much. Only one friend of mine was allowed to come into the house, but to me it was pointless as we weren't allowed to make any noise when my father was in.

I much preferred going to her house, because we could be ourselves and not have to tiptoe around. I was always envious of the relationship my friends had with their fathers and often wished my father and I could have had a similar relationship, but it was not to be. There was no bond between us, and I ended up being terrified of him. I don't ever recall him showing me any affection or telling me that he loved me. My friend's parents invited me to go on holiday with them one year, and I thought to myself there was no way my father would allow it. However, Mum talked him into letting me go and I was over the moon. We were only going to Butlin's holiday camp at Filey on the Yorkshire coast, but it was something to look forward to, plus it meant that I would be having a week away from my father.

It was lovely to spend a whole week with my friend and her parents, as they had a lovely family relationship, which was completely different to what family life was like in my household. They would do lots of things together as a family - days out, and all the fun activities that I longed for within my own family. I was a thirteen-year-old, on holiday with my best friend, having a good time, but I was also worrying about Mum. I would try to put these thoughts to the back of my mind, then suddenly I felt a sick feeling spread across the pit of my stomach as I thought about my mum and wondered if she was okay at home, alone with my father.

Back home, we were living on our nerves, and it was making Mum ill. I longed for the day when I was old enough to start work and get out of that environment once and for all. However, I would not have felt comfortable leaving Mum on her own with him. She always told me that once I was old enough to start work and become independent, we would leave the family home for good - I could not wait!

I left school in 1977, and within a few weeks I had found a job at a factory in my local town. I had just turned sixteen and I was enjoying working. I felt all grown up.

I stood in the wages queue feeling excited. When it was my turn, my first week's wages were handed to me in a small brown envelope that contained the sum of £19.30. I had never had so much money! I felt rich, and I was chuffed to think I would be getting that amount every week. Of course, I had to start paying board and my father had stated how much I had to pay, which was £10 a week. He was giving Mum £10 a week housekeeping and said that I had to pay the same as he was. So, I gave Mum £10 out of my wages and as soon as my father was out of the house, she gave me £5 of it back. Bless her, she said that there was no way she was going to take £10 from me each week, although my father would be led to believe I was paying the full amount. Since I was now working, my father decided that I could stay out in the evening until 10 pm at the weekends, which was better than the 7:30 pm deadline I had been used to.

However, I had started going out with work friends, so I was not prepared to be on a curfew any longer. As far as I was concerned, my father could shove his rules where the sun doesn't shine, which did not go down well. As I was now working, I knew it would only be a matter of time before Mum and I started looking for alternative accommodation. His behaviour was influencing our health, and it had got to the point where we were frightened of our own shadows. Living with this man had affected my schooling, as I was seldom able to concentrate at school due to my home life, and he was now having an effect on my work life. This abusive man had done so much damage, physically and emotionally, and Mum and I were sick of walking on eggshells to avoid annoying him. He ruled the roost, and his behaviour would nowadays be classed as coercive control, which is a criminal offence. It was time to get out for good!

CHAPTER 2

A Fresh Start

A few weeks after I started work, Mum informed me that she had found somewhere else for us to live. I was ecstatic! I hugged Mum while saying, 'Thank you.' It was nothing special, she said, just a small flat, which wasn't far from where I was working.

So, a couple of weeks later, on the Friday, we moved out of the family home into what would become our temporary new home. Unfortunately, I was working on that day, so Mum and one of her friends transported our things from the family home to our new home. My father was at work and had no idea that Mum and I were leaving, so he would be in for a shock when he returned home. We left with very little, just our clothes and a few other bits and bobs, pots and pans, but no furniture as Mum was too frightened to remove any large items from the house.

Mum met me from work so that we could go to our new home together. It was exciting, and I could not wait to get there. The small, two-roomed flat was on the ground floor, and as Mum unlocked the door, I walked in and thought this would do nicely for the time being. It was quiet, and I assumed that the other residents were at work. Everything was upside down as you would expect. There were boxes stacked up by the wall in the kitchen, and numerous bags on the floor in the lounge, but I sat down on the sofa with a huge sigh of relief. We had escaped at last! I could hardly believe it was true. Although the room was unfamiliar, it already felt like home.

Mum and I worked together over the weekend to get things straight. Standing in our new kitchen while taking a break, Mum was smoking a cigarette and staring out of the window. She looked at me as I came into the room and took another cigarette out of the packet. She said casually, 'Would you like a cigarette?' I stood rooted to the spot, shocked at her gesture. I didn't know whether to accept it or not.

Mum said, 'I know that you smoke, so there is no point in hiding it from me anymore. We'll start as we mean to go on.' I took the cigarette and Mum gave me a light. This felt weird as I had never smoked in front of Mum before. I had always been used to smoking in the park or down an alleyway not far from home, or with workmates once I had started working. But this was a fresh start and we both needed to be open about everything, so I smoked in front of Mum from then on. I already knew that she was aware of me smoking because I used to hide a packet of five cigarettes and a book of matches under my bed in the family home. One day, I went upstairs to get them, and they had gone! I was beside myself. I was waiting for Mum to say something about them, but she never did. Obviously, I couldn't say anything to Mum as I shouldn't have been smoking in the first place. It was something that we went on to laugh about years later.

So, we were now living in our new home, which was basic and contained very little. I suppose you could say that it was classed as a semi-furnished flat. We had just two rooms, the lounge/bedroom, and a kitchen. Unfortunately, we had to share the bathroom with other people living in the house, which we weren't too happy about but there was nothing we could do. There was a sofa bed to sit on and a separate single bed positioned in the corner of the room. In the kitchen, there was a cooker, small fridge, and dining table with two chairs. It was cheap and cheerful, but it was clean so it would do for the time being. This was a big step down from our family home, and everything we had been used to, but it was our new home and we had to make the best of it. Both Mum and I knew it would be a struggle, but we would save hard, and in time we would be able to buy new items. We didn't have much, but the one thing we did have was peace of mind. We had escaped, and we felt safe!

Under no circumstances did Mum want my father to find out where we were living as she was so frightened of him. We had to lose contact with the family members and friends we had left behind, because Mum could not risk the chance of them passing on information on our whereabouts to my father. We were enjoying our new-found freedom after being treated like prisoners in our own home for sixteen years. I feel that Mum always regretted not leaving the family home for good sooner than she did, but this was the 1970s and there wasn't the same level of support available for women who suffered domestic violence as there is now.

You got married and you stuck with it, no matter what.

Mum despised the way my father had treated me and always tried to make up for it in the way that I suppose she took on the role of mother and father, and she was brilliant. Mum and I always stuck together, in order to survive. We always felt that united we were stronger. We were so close, and it was a closeness that always remained throughout the years. She never went back to my father and subsequently divorced him.

On my first day at work, I was introduced to Jean who was to show me the ropes. She took me under her wing and trained me up on various jobs on the section where I was working. We bonded instantly and became the best of friends; she was only three years older than me, but I looked up to her. We started going out to pubs and clubs in our local town and occasionally went to Sheffield for a night out.

We were having a great time, and although I was under the legal age for drinking at one point, I never seemed to have a problem getting served at the bar. We were going to discos and nightclubs along with other friends, and I was experiencing a new life. I had lots of lovely work friends, and we always used to meet up on a Friday night to go around town drinking. On a couple of occasions, we went to a nightclub and had to be up early for work the next morning. We must have had some stamina in those days!

Mum had stated that there would be no restrictions now that we had left home. I could go where I wanted and basically do what I wanted as long as I didn't bring any trouble to the door, which I never did. I feel that Mum was trying to make up for the way I had been treated by my father by giving me as much free-dom as I wanted. Mum got on well with all my work mates, and they all liked her. Jean was a regular visitor to our flat. She stayed over occasionally, and we had some good laughs. We did lots of stuff together; she was a great friend, and I loved spending time with her. We were close, and we had some fantastic times together.

One New Year's Eve, Jean and I went to a local club for the evening as there was entertainment on. It was a good night; the drinks were flowing, and I ended up drunk, to the point where I threw up in the back of the taxi on the way home. I'm unable to recall whether Jean was drunk as I was too drunk myself to notice, but it was New Year's Eve after all so I would imagine that she was. I don't remember much about that evening once I had got back home, but I would assume that Mum and Jean put me to bed. That is where I woke up the follow-ing morning with the mother of all hangovers, saying never again.

I thought that I would probably be in trouble from Mum due to the state I had been in the previous night, but she was fine about it. She said that it had been the first New Year's Eve we had spent away from my father, and she was pleased that I had been out with a friend and let my hair down. However, I felt rough for most of New Year's Day. It was the first Christmas and New Year that we had enjoyed, and it was wonderful that Mum had escaped the usual New Year's Eve beat-ing that she got when we were living with my father. I asked her how she was feeling, and she told me that it had been lovely to wake up on New Year's Day without a cut lip, or bruises on her face. I put my arms around her, gave her a hug, and we wished each other 'Happy New Year!'

We stayed at the flat until we could afford to rent a fully furnished house. We did eventually privately rent a house in a different area but didn't stay there long. The house was nice enough, but for some reason neither of us could seem to settle there. There was just something about the house; it had an eerie feeling to it.

Mum had put her name down on the waiting list for a council house, and we were eventually offered a three-bedroom house, which was in a decent area. So, once again we were on the move, only this time it would be a permanent move as we both liked the property and couldn't see a reason why we would ever want to move from there. The house needed furnishing, and Mum had to get a few things on credit from a furniture store in town. We also looked in second-hand furniture shops to obtain certain items, and I can recall Mum finding a nice rug and a coffee table. We had both managed to save some money in anticipation of being offered a property, but it's costly to furnish an entire house. We bought what we could afford at the time and saved hard for the remaining items that we needed.

This was lovely, me and Mum in our own house. We felt happy and relaxed, but most of all we both felt safe. We did see my father in town a couple of times over the years, but he never approached us. Although they were divorced by then, Mum was still fearful of him. Whenever she saw him, she used to become tense and always said, 'That man still has an effect on me.'

Mum and I were enjoying living in our new house and doing all the things that we hadn't been allowed to do when living with my father. This was new-found freedom for us. We were able to come and go as we pleased. My father always said that Mum and I would never make it on our own if ever we left the family home. He couldn't have been more wrong! We were both working, we had our own house, and we had the satisfaction of knowing that, despite all my father's efforts, we were still standing strong, with smiles on our faces. We had done it; we had made a fresh start and a new life for ourselves, and we never looked back!

CHAPTER 3

Meeting John

When I was a young girl, I started to feel as though I was different from some of my friends at school. I wasn't a girly girl; I was more of a tomboy. As I grew up, I felt that I was attracted more to females than males. However, I did have boyfriends, although the relationships never seemed to last long, which was mainly down to me. I don't believe that I ever felt totally comfortable with having a boyfriend, but at the time it seemed the correct thing to do. I remember having nights out with boyfriends, along with workmates, and their partners. We used to have a great time going to the pubs in our local town or maybe going to a club. I was happy enough in male company, but I wasn't bonding with them, relationship-wise.

One evening while I was out with friends, I met John. He was about my height with dark hair and was showing a lot of interest in me. He introduced himself, we started chatting and seemed to be getting on well. He asked me if I would like to meet him one evening for a drink, and I told him that I would love to. A couple of nights later, we met in our local town and went for a drink. It was a quiet night in town, and we managed to find a cosy spot in the pub where we could chat and get to know each other better.

I seemed to get on with him better than I had done with any other boyfriend, so we started dating and our relationship seemed to be going along nicely. After we had been together a couple of weeks, I took him home to meet Mum, and they got on well. I also went to meet John's family, and they were very welcoming. We were getting on fine, and everything in the relationship was good. We had been together for several months and things were just getting better between us. When we weren't working, we always tried to see each other as often as we could, going out for a drink or a meal on a regular basis and just generally enjoying the time we were spending together.

One evening, John suggested booking a holiday as he thought it would be nice for us to spend the week together. At first, I felt slightly nervous about going on holiday with a boyfriend, but there was also a feeling of anticipation in the pit of my stomach. So, we booked our first holiday to Great Yarmouth, a seaside town on the Norfolk coast. Finally, the morning of our departure arrived, and we were filled with excitement, laughing and chatting, as we made our way to the station for what would be a long train journey to our destination.

We were staying in a flat and would eat all our meals out. The weather was glorious, to the point where I foolishly overdid it with the sunbathing and got quite bad sunstroke. I ended up having to spend a couple of days of the holiday in bed, but apart from that we had a brilliant time.

On another occasion, John took me to London for

a long weekend and we stayed with one of his relatives. I had never been to London before, and it was exciting seeing what life was like in this big city. We had a lovely weekend looking at the sights around London, packing in as much as we could, and spending time with members of John's family.

On Saturday evening, as dusk was descending over the Thames, we were walking over Westminster Bridge hand in hand. Suddenly John stopped, turned and looked at me, and said, 'I love you.' It was the first time that he had said it, and although I was quite shocked, it made me feel good. Unfortunately, I couldn't say it back to him as I wasn't in love. I could sense he was disappointed that I hadn't expressed the same words to him, but I just couldn't say them. I loved spending time with him, and I loved the things we did together and the places we went, but he didn't make my heart race, and I certainly wasn't in love with him. I felt that John wanted things to move along within the relationship a lot quicker than I did, which made me feel slightly uneasy.

A few weeks after we had returned home, the relationship started to go downhill, and I suggested a short break from each other. John wasn't too keen at first as he didn't think it was necessary, but I persuaded him that it was for the best. Eventually, he agreed to not having any contact for a couple of weeks, which would give us both plenty of time to decide if the relationship was worth fighting for.

However, within a week, John turned up at the door in tears, saying that his grandmother had passed away. Although we had agreed not to have any contact, he was in such a state that I just couldn't send him away, so I invited him in. I made him a drink, comforted him, and he stayed with me for a couple of hours.

Mum had been out with a friend and was shocked to hear the news about John's grandmother when she returned. She decided to phone his mum to offer our condolences, at which point John said that he needed some air and left. During the phone conversation, Mum was informed that his grandmother hadn't passed away and was in fact alive and well. She passed the information on to me, and I was speechless. I could not believe what John had done or why he had told this appalling lie, but I intended to find out.

His mum was furious and stated that he would be getting a good talking-to when she saw him. I placed myself in that queue, because I needed some answers from him as to why he had resorted to something so low. The following day, I phoned John and asked him to call to see me as I wanted to speak to him. He was reluctant at first, probably because he knew that I was annoyed with him and wanted some answers.

However, he came to see me, and we talked. I asked him why he had told lies about his grandmother, and he admitted that he couldn't cope with us having a break from each other. I pointed out to him that he could have just come and talked to me, rather than resorting to doing what he did. He then turned the tears on and confessed that he thought he was losing me. He had used the story as a way of getting sympathy, with a view to us hopefully getting back together.

It had all been done to get attention, and, if anything, he had made the situation worse. As far as I was concerned, we were no longer on a two-week break, the relationship was over. He asked me why, and I told him that what he had done was unforgivable. I couldn't be in a relationship with someone who would stoop so low to gain attention. I then asked him to leave and reluctantly he did so.

I didn't hear from him for a few days, then one evening he turned up at the door, adamant that he needed to speak to me. I told him calmly that I didn't want to have a conversation with him and asked him to leave. He explained that he wasn't going anywhere until he had said what he had come down to say. He just wanted ten minutes of my time. At that point I invited him in and made it clear that he had five minutes only.

'What do you want, John?' I asked, somewhat impatiently.

'I want to apologise for my behaviour.'

'You were out of order.'

'I know, and I am ashamed of myself,' he replied, with tears in his eyes.

'Why did you say such a thing about your grandmother?' I curiously asked.

'I needed to do something for you to take me back,' was his pathetic reply.

'And is that the best you could come up with?'

'I panicked,' was all that he could say.

'You agreed that we would have a two-week break from each other.'

'I know, but after a week, I started to get concerned because you hadn't contacted me.'

'I didn't contact you, John, because we had agreed to go on a break.' I was now starting to feel frustrated.

'Sorry, but I just couldn't cope with it. I thought I had lost you for good.'

'Your grandmother worships you, and yet you do this to her. God forbid that she ever found out, the shock would probably kill her.'

'I know!' replied John in a quiet voice. 'What I have done is unforgivable, and I couldn't be more sorry or ashamed.'

'Well, that is something you'll have to live with. I have no sympathy for you.'

'So, where does this leave things between us?' he wanted to know.

'I can't be in a relationship with someone who lies to seek attention when things aren't going their way.'

'I made a mistake and nothing like this will ever happen again, I promise.'

'How do I know I can trust you?'

'I swear I will be totally honest with you if you take me back.'

'I'm not sure whether that's a risk I can afford to take.'

John looked into my eyes and said, 'Look, I love you and I want this to work. We are good together. Please don't let one mistake ruin our relationship for good. I'm not likely to do anything else that will jeopardise the relationship, am I?'

'I suppose not,' I replied reluctantly.

'So, will you take me back?'

I paused for a while, staring out of the window. I didn't know how to respond. Eventually, I said, 'I'm not prepared to make that decision at this moment. I need time to think. I don't know if I can trust you anymore.'

'You can trust me, and I will prove it to you if you give me the chance.'

'Give me some time and I'll get back to you.'

'When will you let me know?'

'I'll give you a call tomorrow,' I promised.

'Fine! I do love you and I am sincerely sorry for what I've done. It will never happen again; you have my word.'

'Like I said, I'll let you know.' I was struggling to hold back the tears. I just wanted him to leave.

'Okay and thank you for listening to me,' he said as he made his way to the front door.

'I'll be in touch,' was all I could say as I closed the door behind him.

I had a lot of serious thinking to do. I knew he was genuinely sorry for what he had done, but I was concerned that there may be a recurrence in the future. Should I break away now, or should I give him a second chance? After all, it wasn't as though I was madly in love with him, but I did enjoy being with him and I assumed the 'love' part of the relationship would happen for me at some point. I didn't know what to do for the best.

After sleeping on it and speaking to Mum, I decided to give him a second chance. I wanted a 100% guarantee that he would not lie to me again, and that he would never pull another stunt like that. He agreed and said that he couldn't believe I was willing to continue with the relationship. I told him not to get his hopes up of the relationship being permanent as he was on a two-week trial, and if things went okay within that time, we would talk further. He agreed, although I didn't give him a choice. It was on those terms or nothing.

So, we were back together, and he was doing everything he possibly could to make up for what he had done, and our relationship was good again. The two-week period came to an end, and I was satisfied that he had changed his ways and hadn't lied to me again, at least to my knowledge. I told him I would be happy for the relationship to continue, and he breathed a sigh of relief. I also pointed out that if he continued in the way he had been doing for the previous two weeks, I didn't envisage any further problems.

Our relationship seemed to go from strength to strength. He was behaving himself and being attentive to me, which was nice in small doses, but I was starting to find it a touch irritating. We didn't see each other every night as we both felt that there should be at least a couple of nights a week when we were able to do our own thing if we chose to. However, on the nights when we saw each other, John would often turn up with a box of chocolates or a bunch of flowers. One evening I said, 'The flowers are lovely, and I appreciate them, but you don't need to keep buying me gifts each time you come round.'

'But I don't want to lose you,' he replied, looking

into my eyes.

'As long as you're honest with me, there won't be a problem.'

'I am being honest,' he said earnestly, 'I promise I will always be honest with you.'

'Well, that's all I want from you,' I concluded.

Months passed, and all seemed to be going well within the relationship. I was pleased that I had decided to give him a second chance to prove himself to me. We were both enjoying the relationship and doing all the things that young couples do when they are together, and just generally going out and having a good time. However, Friday night was always the girls' night out in town, so I didn't see John, unless it was for one drink in the last pub we went into. It was different on a Saturday evening as John and I always went out together, sometimes for a meal, or just for a drink with friends, and he would regularly stay over. Mum would always invite him to stay for Sunday lunch. He loved Mum's roast dinners, and the fact that she always piled his plate up was a bonus. There was always plenty of meat, vegetables, a mountain of potatoes, and as many Yorkshire puddings as John could eat. He used to devour the lot and always left a clean plate.

By now, my feelings for John had started to get stronger, to the point where I thought that I could say I loved him. Still, something was holding me back from saying it, but I wasn't sure what. Time went on and I did eventually get around to telling John that I loved him, and he was thrilled. His face lit up, he threw his arms around me, and hugged me. However, he did point out that it had taken me long enough to say it. Although I had said the words he wanted to hear, somehow it didn't feel right. He made me laugh, he was kind and generous - there were many things that I liked about him, but there were also things that I didn't want to have to tolerate within the relationship. We were young and still getting to know each other, and only time would tell whether the relationship was for keeps.

CHAPTER 4

Celebrations

We had been going out for around eighteen months, and as far as I was aware, John was being honest with me. One evening, he came round, and we decided to watch TV upstairs. We didn't have to. Mum was always happy for us to sit downstairs with her, but sometimes we wanted to talk in private, so spending time in my bedroom was the obvious choice.

We were lying on the bed talking when suddenly John looked at me and said, 'Marry me.' Immediately, panic set in and I thought, *Oh my God, I didn't see this coming.* I couldn't get any words out to answer him and rushed downstairs to make a drink.

When I returned to the bedroom, he said, 'Well I didn't expect that response.'

'What do you want me to say, John?' I asked.

'Yes would have been nice,' he replied, somewhat sullenly.

When I didn't say anything, he took hold of my hands and looked straight into my eyes. Silence reigned for a few moments. Then, he said in a quiet voice, 'It's just that I love you so much, and I want us to be together, always.'

'I'm sorry,' I replied, looking down at the pattern on the carpet. 'I just need some time to think about it.'

I was shocked at his proposal as it appeared to come out of nowhere, and it wasn't something we had ever discussed. I needed time to consider whether it was what I wanted. There had been times when John had lied to me, and from past experience I knew that he could be unpredictable. I needed time to digest his proposal, and to his disappointment, I wasn't prepared to give him an answer that night.

A few days later, we went out for a meal. While we were eating, John asked me if I could give him an answer to his proposal. I promised I would put him out of his misery once we had finished eating. So, the plates were cleared, we both had a drink in our hands, and I said, 'Yes, I will marry you.'

A broad smile appeared on his face. He leaned across the table, kissed me and said, 'You have made me so happy.'

The following weekend, we went out looking at engagement rings. He bought me a beautiful ring with sapphires and diamonds, and we got engaged on my twenty-first birthday. He had booked a table at a lovely intimate restaurant in town and gave me the engagement ring while we were there. The manager congratulated us and brought two glasses of champagne to our table. The following day, I received a lovely bouquet of flowers that John had ordered for me, and in the evening, a party had been arranged at a local venue to celebrate my birthday, which we now combined with our engagement.

I was chuffed to bits, and everyone wanted to admire my engagement ring, which I was more than happy to show as it was beautiful, and I was proud of it. It had been a lovely weekend with so much to celebrate, and we had received some beautiful gifts. Thinking back, that had been an expensive weekend for family and friends. Not only did they buy birthday presents for me, they also bought gifts for our engagement. We were both happy. I had turned twenty-one, and John and I had got engaged - life was good!

As the evening went on, I couldn't understand why John's mum and other members of his family hadn't arrived at the venue to celebrate our engagement with us, but I intended to find out. The next day, I told John that I was going to phone his mum to find out why she and other family members hadn't joined us the previous evening to celebrate my birthday, and our engagement. He promised he would speak to her when he got home and said there was no need for me to phone her. I maintained that I would like to speak to her myself. At that point, John decided to go for a walk to clear his head as he had had a lot to drink the previous evening.

While he was out, I phoned his mum to ask if she was okay and why she hadn't turned up to our engagement party the previous evening. Her reply was, 'I didn't know you and John had got engaged.' I was furious, to say the least! How could John have done this to his own mum? He hadn't even mentioned it to her, or any of his family. Worse was to come. She said that I had made a big mistake getting engaged to him because he would end up hurting me. Her words made my heart sink. I started to feel upset. I didn't know what to say. She wondered where John was, and I informed her that he had gone for a walk, but I would be speaking to him when he returned.

While pacing the floor, I eagerly waited for John to reappear. Finally, an hour later, John sauntered in. I asked him if there was anything that he wanted to tell me, as I needed some answers regarding the discussion I had just had with his mum on the phone. Of course, he didn't have anything to say. He just stood there with a cocky look on his face. I needed to find out what game he was playing, and why he hadn't wanted his mum and other family members at the party, so I questioned him.

'Why didn't you tell your mum that we were getting engaged?'

'Oh, I thought I had,' he replied.

'Crap!' I said in a stern voice.

'I'm sure I told her,' he claimed.

'Well, your mum is certain that you didn't,' I quickly replied.

'I was going to tell her, but then I forgot.'

'You forgot?'

'Yes, sorry.'

'John, it's not the sort of thing that you would forget to tell your own mother.'

'What's the problem? We had a good night.'

'Yes, we did have a good night, but your mum and other family members should have been there to celebrate with us.'

'Well, we've been having quite a few arguments, so I didn't really want her to go.'

'She was in tears when I came off the phone because she hadn't been included.'

'I'm sorry, I'll make it up to her.'

'I felt so sorry for your mum. Her son and his girlfriend have just got engaged and yet she wasn't a part of the celebrations.'

'I've not lied to you; I just didn't tell her.'

'I don't know which is worse.'

'Are we okay?'

'I suppose so, but you need to talk to your mum and make things right with her.'

At that point, he gathered his things together and shuffled towards the front door.

He came back later that day and told me that he had had a good talk with his mum and apologised to her. He also promised to take her out for a nice meal to make it up to her. His mum phoned me and confirmed that John had spoken to her and apologised. She then suggested that I keep her up to date with future developments as John couldn't be relied on to keep her informed.

Afterwards, some comments that John's mum had made on the phone were niggling at me so much that I decided I needed to have a further talk with her. So, I arranged to go to see her a couple of days later. I arrived at her house while John was at work, and we had a long chat. She reiterated what she had previously said, and I asked her to elaborate. With a sigh, she admitted that John had lied to her on numerous occasions over certain events in the past, and I pointed out that he had also lied to me. I also mentioned that he was supposed to have changed his ways, though I was now starting to question that. She hoped he had changed, otherwise he would end up ruining our marriage. I reassured her that I felt confident that everything would be okay.

Now that we were engaged, we needed to start making plans and saving for our future. John wanted to start looking for a house to buy at some point, so any spare bit of money we had went straight into our savings account. We decided to cut back on nights out and going out for meals, as we felt that the money we would save would help towards buying a house and paying for our wedding. Both John and I were working full time and earning good money so we knew that we would be able to afford to take on a mortgage. We had done our sums and worked out that everything would be fine. Weeks went on and we decided to start looking for a house with a view to making a purchase. What an eye-opener that was; it's surprising what some people will say to try to sell their house.

For one house, the details stated that the property had been newly decorated throughout with a good-sized kitchen and bathroom, so we decided to go and view it. Oh my God! We walked in and were met with a musty smell. The walls had been papered, but in some parts, the paper was starting to peel away. The house was so damp, if there had been a fire in there, I'm sure it would have put itself out. And as for the good-sized kitchen, I'm sure I could see scratch marks on the walls where someone had been trying to swing a cat. We went upstairs to view the bedrooms and bathroom, and they were all far too small, at which point we informed them that we had seen enough; it wasn't what we were looking for. We couldn't have lived there; it was depressing. So, we needed to keep looking for a suitable property. We did eventually find a house we liked. It was a two-bedroom terraced house, with a decent-sized kitchen and bathroom. I was particularly drawn to the fireplace in the lounge as it had light-coloured brickwork surrounding it. Feeling nervous and excited at the same time, we put in an offer, and it was accepted.

We started making plans for our wedding and continued buying items for the bottom drawer. Ha ha! I doubt the young ones of today would have a clue what the term 'bottom drawer' meant! It used to be the place where young women would keep towels, bedding, and other items they would use after marriage. By now, we had managed to save quite a bit of money which we knew would be desperately needed, because there would be a house to furnish once the sale had gone through. We needed to concentrate on sorting the house out first, but we wouldn't be able to afford all the furniture at once. However, as long as we had bought all the necessary household items, we could build things up as we went along. The couple selling the house were already in their new property, and we were first-time buyers so there wouldn't be any hold-ups and the sale would go through quite quickly.

I personally felt that things were moving too fast. We had got engaged, and we were now in the process of buying a house together and making wedding plans, all within a matter of months. Thoughts like, *Am I happy? Is this what I really want? Do I want to commit?* swirled around my head. Something didn't feel right, there were lots of things I was unsure of, and I felt suffocated.

From start to finish, it took around eight weeks for us to get the keys to our first home. We didn't move in straight away as there were a few things we wanted to do to the property first. We cleaned the house from top to bottom, as you do, then we decided to do some decorating, or should I say we attempted to, in the form of wallpapering. Neither of us had ever done any wallpapering before. I had done some painting in the past and thought wallpapering shouldn't be too difficult, so we were both prepared to get stuck in and give it a go. Can I just say that no matter how well you think you know your partner, until you've attempted to do some decorating with them, you don't know them at all. It didn't go too well; all we did was argue, so we ended up getting someone in to decorate for us. We also had some new internal doors fitted and one or two other jobs done.

We had new flooring laid downstairs and took delivery of a new suite and various other furniture items. One of John's relatives worked in the furniture department at the Co-op store in town and managed to get us a good discount on our new suite. My mum bought us a washing machine as an early wedding present and John's mum bought us a lovely coffee table. Everything was starting to come together, and it was looking homely. We had lovely neighbours on one side. They were older than us and were a nice couple. We became quite friendly with them and had the odd night out together, or they would come around to our house for drinks. The lady at the other side was okay, but she could be quite nosey and gossiped a lot. She was alright to pass the time of day with, but that was it. It felt rather strange at first, not living with Mum, but John and I had moved into our new home together and would soon be getting married. Having our own home took a bit of getting used to. Although we were fine as a couple, living together felt quite awkward for both of us, and we had to get into a new routine.

One piece of good advice Mum gave me was to always pay our bills on time, which we did, and I still do. I think that I found living together more difficult than John did. He had regularly stayed over at Mum's in the past but that was completely different from living together. For a start, we had separate bedrooms when he stayed over, so I had to get used to sharing a bed with him. On the first night in our new home, I felt like a fish out of water. I was missing Mum and started to wonder if we had done the right thing in signing up to buy a house. Maybe we should have just rented somewhere. We were both in our early twenties and having our own house and a mortgage seemed like a huge commitment. I had flown the nest, and it was the worst feeling ever. However, this was our new way of life, and something that I had to get used to.

CHAPTER 5

Getting Married

We were now planning our wedding, and as anyone who has ever been married will know, there is an awful lot of preparation involved. We were both working full time, so a lot of things had to be organised in the evening or at weekends. We set the date, which was to be 2nd June 1984, just before my twenty-third birthday. All things wedding related were starting to come together and we were looking forward to the big day. I had made an appointment at a bridal shop in town, accompanied by Mum. I think all girls want their mum to be with them when choosing their wedding dress. I looked at various styles and eventually chose a dress to try on. I walked out of the fitting room in a beautiful snow-white dress with long sleeves and a high neck-line. I felt like a princess. As soon as Mum saw me, she started to cry and said that I looked beautiful. I had a feeling that we were going to go through a lot of tissues that day, luckily there was a box to hand.

I asked Mum her opinion on the length of the dress and the design, and she assured me that everything about the dress was perfect. However, I didn't make a decision that day as I wanted to return for a second fitting, just to be certain. A week later, I went back to the bridal shop, tried the dress on again and felt certain that this was the dress for me. Mum agreed. I paid a deposit, and both Mum and I were thrilled I had finally chosen the dress I would be walking down the aisle in. The bridesmaid's dresses had been ordered, and John and his brother, who was to be his best man, had bought their suits. Mum had chosen her outfit - a pale grey two-piece, which she would wear with a white blouse and matching accessories. We had so many laughs when she was looking for a hat. She wasn't very tall, and no matter which style of hat she tried on, nothing seemed to suit her. She wasn't a hat person, but she did eventually find the perfect one which complemented her outfit.

The ceremony was to be performed at my local church, and the reception was being held at a hotel in town. The hotel was undergoing extensive refurbishment at the time of booking, but we were assured by the management that they would be up and running for our wedding day. We made several pre-wedding visits to the hotel to discuss our requirements and pricing, and at one point we had concerns as to whether the refurbishment works would be completed, and the hotel would re-open in time for our wedding reception.

The date of our wedding was nearing, yet the hotel still hadn't re-opened. I was starting to panic and was beginning to wish that we had booked an alternative venue. However, it did open as promised, and we went along to have a grand tour. It was beautiful inside, and everything was fresh and new. Along with having our reception there, we had also booked a room overnight. The hotel manager invited us to return to the hotel for a complimentary first anniversary meal, which of course we accepted. It would have been rude not to!

Finally, the day of the wedding arrived, and it was a glorious day, the sun was shining, and everyone was in good spirits. There was a knock at the door. As I opened the door, a delivery man handed me a beautiful bouquet of flowers that John had ordered for me.

I was nervous, as you would expect; it was my wedding day. There was an endless stream of people in and out of Mum's. We were all busy doing something wedding related, and the kettle was permanently on. I got into a panic at one point, as the hoops which were to be inserted into my dress to make it stand out from the waist down would not go in properly, so everyone was helping and concentrating on this task. Finally, we managed to put them in correctly. I was ready to get married, or so I thought! A wave of doubt came over me and I started to question whether getting married was what I wanted to do, although this was a fine time to be having second thoughts.

'Mum, I don't feel happy about going through with this.'

'What's wrong sweetheart?' she replied, in a concerned voice.

'I'm not sure this is what I want.'

'You need to be 100% certain before you walk down the aisle,' Mum stated.

'I feel that John has put too much pressure on me to get married,' I replied as tears welled up in my eyes.

'You don't need to go through with this if your feelings of doubt are so strong.'

'It's probably just wedding day nerves,' I quickly replied.

'You wouldn't be the first bride to have these feelings on her wedding day,' she reassured me.

'I need to pull myself together and get a grip. I'll be fine,' I said apprehensively.

Time was getting on, the wedding car would be on its way, and John and our guests would be waiting for me at the church. I felt that I couldn't let them down. When a beautiful white Cadillac arrived, I made my way outside. As expected, quite a few of the neighbours were out, which often happens when a wedding car pulls up on the street as everyone likes to admire a bride in her wedding dress. So, I was on my way to the church to get married.

It was only a short drive away. In fact, to be honest, I could have walked round, but a bride walking to church on her wedding day is just not done. I had three bridesmaids, - two adults and one toddler. My chief bridesmaid was my best friend, the second adult bridesmaid was an old school friend, and the toddler was the daughter of a close friend who I worked with. She looked so cute in her little white dress, like a mini bride carrying a basket of flowers - bless her! She was only two years old when I got married. She is now in her thirties and has grown into a beautiful young woman.

Everyone looked gorgeous in their wedding attire. Mum looked stunning in her outfit, and I was so proud of her. I am not a parent myself so I have never known the feeling of seeing a daughter get married, although I can imagine that it is a feeling of mixed emotions. Parents are probably happy to see you moving on in life, but also sad because they are losing part of their baby girl.

The marriage ceremony took place. While John and I were exchanging vows, I knew in my heart that the marriage would never last. Following the photographs, we all headed to the reception venue. We were met with a glass of champagne, and the camera was pointed in our direction again. We then made our way into the dining room where a three-course meal was to be served. The room looked beautiful; great attention to detail had been made in decorating the tables. The food was delicious, and we had received some thoughtful wedding gifts from family and friends. In the evening, we danced at a disco until around midnight. John led me out onto the dance floor for the first dance. It had been a long day, but thankfully, everything had gone smoothly and to plan.

I was now a married woman and ready to start married life - or so I thought! We had been living together, so nothing had changed apart from having a wedding ring on my finger and a piece of paper stating that our relationship was official. We were getting on well and enjoying married life.

We had started going out to a local club on a Saturday evening and one evening, when we were ordering drinks at the bar, a couple invited us to sit with them. We had seen them in the club before but hadn't spoken to them. They introduced themselves as Chris and Martin. They were a nice couple, and quite chatty. Chris and

I hit it off from the word go; we just seemed to click. We started to meet them each weekend in the club and became good friends. We had some good nights out and occasionally we would all go out for a meal.

Within our marriage, things seemed good at first as you would expect when you are newly married, but that was short-lived, and it wasn't long before cracks started to appear. It's surprising how a marriage certificate can change someone, and things did change - dramatically!

Everything had been fine between us when we were engaged otherwise I would never have got married, but within a few weeks of marriage, John had completely changed. In fact, I had never seen such a rapid transformation within a person. He went from being the attentive, fun-loving fiancé to someone who wasn't happy unless he was getting his own way. If we had still been engaged, it would have been so much easier to walk away from the relationship, but it's a bit more difficult when you are married, as there are a lot more factors to consider.

We were having a lot of arguments, and seemed to easily get on each other's nerves, to the point where we couldn't bear to be in the same room together for long periods of time. It appeared that everything I did irritated John and vice versa, so I would spend time at Mum's to alleviate the monotony. I wasn't bonding well with the house either, in the way that I could not seem to settle there. It was a nice house, but there was something about it that didn't feel right, and I just couldn't warm to it.

Our marriage wasn't going well at all; John had

started lying to me again and he was creating a lot of problems. I had a wedding ring on my finger, a marriage certificate, and I felt trapped. We decided to have a good long talk to try and get our marriage back on track.

'You've changed so much, John.'

'So you keep saying,' was his reply.

'You have no idea how much damage you're doing to this marriage,' I retorted.

'So what would you like me to do?' he said, sarcastically.

'Stop lying to me and being so demanding,' I insisted.

'I'll sort myself out,' he assured me.

'I do hope so John, otherwise there is no point in staying together.'

'I don't want the marriage to end,' he quickly replied.

'You weren't demanding before we got married, and there is no need for it now.'

I made it clear that he wasn't going to get his own way all the time - there had to be give and take within the marriage. He promised me that he would change, so we carried on with the marriage and things did change - but not for long! So, it was back to the drawing board, and we had another long chat. I asked him if he still wanted to be married and he declared that he did. I reminded him that the change had been short-lived and that we were now back at square one.

'You just can't see what you're doing wrong can

you, John?'

'Not this again,' he answered.

Your behaviour is putting our marriage at risk,' I reminded him.

'I'm going out for a drink,' he announced, as he walked out of the lounge and marched down the hallway.

'Maybe we shouldn't have got married and just stayed as we were,' I shouted.

'Why do you say that?' he asked, as he walked back into the lounge.

'Things were fine when we were engaged.'

'Things are fine now, as far as I'm concerned,' was his reply.

'I can't continue living like this, and I'm not prepared to,' I firmly told him.

'Do you still love me?' he asked.

'I'm not sure, John,' was all I could say to him.

John walked out of the house and slammed the door behind him.

I loved him as a friend, but I didn't feel that I was 'in love' with him. At the time we got married, I thought I was in love, but did I even know what love was? I certainly knew that you wouldn't treat someone you loved the way he was now treating me. Even on the morning of our wedding, doubts about whether I wanted to go through with the ceremony had swirled through my head.

I enjoyed his company when things were going

well between us, but that wasn't enough to save the marriage, and looking back I don't feel that I was ever in love with him. It seemed such a shame, all things considered, as we had spent a lot of money on the wedding. Not only that, we had both signed up for the mortgage and I just felt that there was no way out. The marriage wasn't working. He had placed a wedding ring on my finger, and he had completely changed. Everything within the marriage felt wrong and it wasn't how I envisaged married life to be.

We hadn't fallen out; we just didn't know which way to go with the marriage. The one person I should have listened to before getting married was John's mother. She tried to talk me out of marrying him and claimed that he would end up hurting me. But I was young, and like a lot of young people, I thought I knew it all, so I took no notice whatsoever of her advice. Looking back, I realise that she had my best interests at heart, and I wish I had listened to her. I also felt that getting married at the age of twenty-two was far too young and had been a huge mistake.

I always got on well with John's mum; we were good friends, but her son was such a liar. He would go to work and state a time when he would be home, and I used to get a meal ready for that time, but regularly he would turn up one or two hours later, saying that he had been working late. When he came in the door he reeked of alcohol, but he insisted that he hadn't been drinking, which used to annoy me. If he wanted to have a drink after work, then I didn't object. What I did object to was him lying about it. The same thing happened repeatedly, and one evening it was after 9 pm when he finally turned up. Again, there was a distinct smell of alcohol, and when I asked him where he had been, he told me that he had been working late. 'You're lying!' I retorted, but he insisted that was where he had been. I said, 'Okay, we'll leave it at that.' I wasn't prepared to get into a full-blown argument.

Most of the time, I knew when John was lying. Apart from the obvious, his lips moving, I knew all the tell-tale signs: the look in his eyes and the way he used to become fidgety when he was struggling for answers. He was lying to me and wasting money that we couldn't afford to waste. We were both working hard and earning good money, but we had a mortgage to pay and all the usual household bills. We were okay for money, but we didn't have enough to be wasting it. I wasn't wasting money, and I needed to make sure that John wasn't wasting money on alcohol night after night. Weeks went by and we decided to give the marriage one final chance. We agreed that if it failed to improve, we would separate. It wasn't what either of us wanted, but we knew that it would be the only option as we could not go on like this indefinitely.

By now, Mum had sensed that something was not quite right within the marriage, but I didn't go into too much detail because I didn't want her worrying. I told her that we were having a few problems but were working on them and hopefully our relationship was going to improve. We started having 'date nights' which we enjoyed, and things seemed to start picking up. I thought, at last, we were getting our marriage back on track. I had seen a change for the better in John, and he assured me that things would continue to improve over the coming weeks. I told him that they needed to, otherwise there would be no point in us staying together. I emphasised that this was his last chance and if things went wrong again, we would be looking at splitting up. Weeks went by and all seemed well. He was making a real effort and the relationship was back to how it was when we were engaged - for now!

I was still working full time, but I hated the job. John suggested that I handed my notice in if the job was making me feel so miserable. I thought that we wouldn't be able to afford our expenses if I left work, but he claimed that it wouldn't be a problem as he had had a pay rise, and there was also plenty of overtime on offer. He also said that I would end up leaving work anyway when we started a family. We had discussed starting a family, but John had changed so much, and at that time I didn't feel that I wanted to have children with him. The relationship wasn't stable enough, and I felt that bringing a child into that environment would have been the wrong thing to do.

We sat down, did some sums and worked out that we wouldn't be that much worse off if I did stop working, plus I would look for a new part-time job. So, I handed my notice in and to be honest I was glad to see the back of the place. I had stuck it out for seven years and I had had enough of it. The girls I worked with were brilliant and ended up being some of the best friends I have ever had, but the work was boring, so I was glad to be away from it. I informed Mum that I had handed my notice in at work, and she went mad.

'What the hell do you think you're doing?' she asked.

'Mum, the job was getting me down,' I replied.

'You've just taken on a mortgage for God's sake.'

'We've worked things out and we'll be okay for money.'

'Well, I do hope so, but I think you're taking a risk.'

'I'm going to look for a part-time job, it will be fine,' I assured her.

'I'm your mum, and I'll never stop worrying about you,' she said, hugging me.

I felt happier once I had left my job as it had been getting me down for some time. It was nice to be feeling less stressed. As I would now be spending a lot more time in the house, I hoped I would start to feel more comfortable there, but time would tell. I would also see more of Mum, as she would come down and spend the day with me, and I would cook lunch for us both, or I would go to Mum's, and John would join us after he had finished work. He liked my mum, but her feelings towards him took a slide after we got married because she could see how unhappy he was making me.

When things were good between us, we couldn't have been happier, but it always seemed to be short-lived, and it was never long before things went downhill again. I didn't want to be living in an environment where there were frequent arguments or long silences. I had witnessed enough of that as a child, and I certainly wasn't prepared to tolerate it within my own marriage. However, I could see that John was trying hard to mend his ways and our marriage started to improve. He was less demanding, and he seemed to have reverted to how he was when we were engaged. I felt happier than I had for a while, but over the coming weeks I saw a side to John that I had never seen before, which gave me a great deal of cause for concern.

CHAPTER 6

A New Direction

We continued going to our local club at the weekend and meeting up with Chris and Martin most Saturday evenings. Occasionally, they would come back to our house for a drink at the end of the night. This went on for months and we became great friends.

We used to have the odd game of pool during the evening, and one time when John and I were having a game, it was my turn to take a shot. As I was leaning over the pool table to focus on the ball I was about to hit, I could sense that Chris was watching me. I met her gaze and saw that she was looking at me in a way she had never looked at me before. Consequently, this was off-putting, so I missed my shot and lost the game - which I wasn't too happy about. The evening carried on, and we were all having a good time, though I couldn't get the image out of my mind of how Chris had looked at me earlier as it had made me feel uncomfortable. It was the kind of look that you give someone when you have feelings for them. I'm quite smart in that respect and pick up on body language easily. However, nothing was said about it before the evening ended.

The following weekend, we met as usual and during the short time we were in their company, I observed intermittent glances from Chris. We didn't stay out with them for long on this occasion as John and I had made arrangements to go into town for a meal. We left it a couple of weeks before going back to the club. As we walked in, I noticed that our friends weren't there, which was unusual because they would normally have been in at that time. I thought, *Oh my God, this is awful, they're not here. I'm going to have to put up with John all night, on my own!* What a jolly night that was - NOT! I couldn't understand why they hadn't turned up as they had said they would be there. I wondered if maybe Chris had realised that the way she had looked at me had been out of order, and that she was now embarrassed and avoiding me. I was confused, yet disappointed that they hadn't turned up as they were good company, and we always had a great evening.

The following week, they were sitting at their usual table when we walked in. Apparently, they had both been unwell the previous week. We had a good night at the club and Chris asked for our phone number, so she could let us know in future if they weren't going to be there. Later that evening, they came back to our home for a drink, and we chatted while music was playing softly in the background. When they left, as usual we hugged and said goodnight, though the hug I received from Chris was different from previous hugs she had given me. Some people may say that a hug is a hug, but I disagree. I feel that there are different types of hugs for different people. The hug Chris gave me that night certainly wasn't what you would expect from a friend. It seemed to linger and was akin to a hug you would have with your partner. It felt good, but at the same time I thought, *What the hell is going on here?* While she was hugging me, she said softly, 'I'll call you.' I went to bed and all I could think about was how Chris had been with me, and how it had made me feel. It was as though she just didn't want to let go once she started hugging me.

My emotions were all over the place, things were happening that I just couldn't handle, and it was scaring me. I hardly got any sleep that night as I was unable to switch off from what had happened. I had this image in my mind of how the hug had been and started to wonder if the situation had meant something to me. I needed to get my head around what was happening because I felt that things were moving in a direction that I was unsure of. We had both had quite a bit to drink, so I wondered if I had misread the way she had been looking at me, and her mannerisms towards me. I kept asking myself, *Did I misread the whole situation?* I was so confused.

The following day, I was unable to concentrate on anything and I could not get that hug out of my mind. I decided we needed to keep our distance from each other. I wanted some space, so I didn't go out with them for the following couple of weeks. By this time, we had become close friends, and Chris had sensed that something wasn't right. She phoned me and asked why I wasn't going out. I informed her that I hadn't felt up to it as I had a few things on my mind, so we left it at that, and had no contact with each other.

Christmas came around, and I knew we wouldn't be going out over the festive period as we would be spending time with family, which is what we did each year. Over Christmas, things started to slide again in our marriage, and I could see that John was slipping back into his old ways - watch this space! Once Christmas was over, Chris rang to invite us out on New Year's Eve, and I told her that I would get back to her and let her know. I was unsure what I wanted to do at first, because I didn't know how things would be between me and John. I asked him if he wanted to go, but he wasn't bothered either way. I stated that I was going as I didn't want to stay in on New Year's Eve. He then decided he would go, since he didn't want to be at home on his own. I told him that if he was coming out with me, he needed to be on his best behaviour, which of course he always was while we were out. It was usually when we got home that he changed!

We met early at our usual club in order to get a table as it was likely to become busy on New Year's Eve. We walked in and saw Chris and Martin waiting for us. Chris looked at me and gave me a lovely smile. It was good to see her, and I realised that we had made the correct decision in going out. There was music playing and everyone was in good spirits, just as you would expect on New Year's Eve. We were dancing, having a good time, and the evening just seemed to fly by. Midnight approached and there was the usual countdown to the New Year. Everyone was wishing each other 'Happy New Year' and kissing their respective partners, including John and me. He put his arms around me and said, 'A new year, a new start, things will be different.'

I wished Chris 'Happy New Year.' She gave me a hug, kissed me on the cheek and said, 'Happy New Year,

Sweetheart.' I thought to myself, *Sweetheart! What's that all about?*

We had all been invited back to someone's house for a party, just up the road from where we lived, so we left the club and made our way to the party. Everyone was enjoying themselves. We were quite merry, but we weren't drunk. I decided to pop home to get some of my music, and Chris said she would come with me. At home, I started looking through my collection while asking Chris's opinion on which music to select.

'This is the first time we've had the opportunity to be alone this evening,' Chris suddenly said.

'It's been a good evening, though,' I commented.

'Are you okay?' she enquired, with a look of concern.

'I'm fine.'

'Are you sure? Because something is telling me that you're not. I know that John is getting to you.'

'I don't want to discuss it at the moment,' I stated, while handing her a record.

'I'm always here if you need to talk,' she offered.

'I know.'

'I enjoyed the hug we had last time I was here,' she revealed, smiling at me.

'It was just a hug,' I nervously replied.

'Being so close to you felt good,' she declared.

I thought, *God, I'm not prepared for this.* I needed another drink. I went into the kitchen and poured us both a drink and we stood talking.

'How did it make you feel?'

'I'm unsure of my feelings, though it was different to previous hugs,' I admitted.

'There's something I need to tell you.'

'What's that?' I asked.

At that point, the front door opened, and John walked in. The look on Chris's face changed and she whispered, 'Lousy timing.' I picked up my glass and walked out, while Chris remained in the kitchen. To be honest, I thought his timing had been perfect because had he walked in a minute later, I feel that he would have walked in on a completely different situation. He had wondered if everything was okay as we had been gone a while. We finished our drinks, gathered up the music we had selected, and went back with John.

Towards the end of the party, slow songs were being played, and John wanted me to dance with him. I found it funny how suddenly he wanted to start getting close to me, which I knew for a fact was because he would want to have sex when we got home. He didn't have a snowball's chance in hell. *It's not happening matey - jog on!* I thought. Not long after that, we left, as it was 3 am.

When we got home, John went to pour a drink and asked me if I would like one. I declined as I had had enough, but he still went ahead and poured me one. I left it lying on the table. He wanted to know why I wouldn't dance with him at the party, and I revealed that I knew what his game was. He looked at me and declared that he wanted to make love. I told him it wasn't happening - I would be sleeping in the spare room. A couple of minutes later he went upstairs, and I thought he had gone to bed, but then he appeared back in the lounge. 'I'm off to bed. Don't forget to turn the lights off,' I reminded him, as I made a quick exit.

I walked into the spare room and in the middle of the floor was a pile of bedding. He had stripped the bed so that I would sleep in the same bed as him. I went back downstairs to find out why he had done it, but he wouldn't answer me. He was always the same when he had been drinking and he hadn't got his own way. I made it clear that I would be making the bed back up and that was where I would be sleeping. To be honest, I would have slept on the floor rather than share a bed with him. 'You have been turning me on all night and I want to make love to you,' he revealed. I informed him that those feelings weren't reciprocated, and I went to bed. I was foolish to think I was going to get any sleep. A few minutes after I had gone upstairs, John put some music on, which was louder than it should have been at that time in the morning. I got up, went back downstairs, reminded him what time it was and that we had neighbours either side of us. 'I couldn't care less,' he retorted. 'It's my house and I can do what I like.' I turned the music off and suggested that he went to bed.

He got up from the sofa, walked into the kitchen and banged his glass down onto the worktop. It smashed. Shards of glass went everywhere. 'For God's sake, John, just go to bed, you've had enough to drink, you need some sleep,' I said. He went to bed, and I went back upstairs a few minutes later. He hadn't got his own way and that's what all the banging about downstairs was in aid of. He was so childish.

We got up around lunch time, and I will admit that I wasn't feeling at my best, but it had been New Year's Eve after all. Our spirits were high, and we had all had a brilliant evening, until we got home. When I walked into the lounge, John was sitting on the sofa with a cup of tea in his hand, and you could have cut the atmosphere with a knife. I looked at him and I could tell that he wasn't in the best of moods. He questioned why I hadn't picked the broken pieces up from when he had smashed his glass, and I said that I wasn't clearing up after him. If he had smashed the glass accidently, I would have cleaned it up, but not when he had smashed it deliberately. He could clean his own mess up.

'Why did you sleep in the spare room?' he asked.

I ignored him.

'Is it going to become a regular thing?'

'It's going to be permanent, John.'

'Why?'

'I'm sick of you acting the way you do whenever you've been drinking. You've run out of chances. I'm not putting up with your behaviour any longer,' I retorted.

'So what are you saying?'

'We're finished. The marriage is over.'

'We can sort this out,' he insisted.

'The marriage isn't working, and I'm sick of papering over the cracks,' I replied.

'Let's talk about it,' he suggested.

'No, John, I've had enough.'

'Don't do this to me,' he pleaded.

'I'm not prepared to keep living this way. It's over.'

Everything around me was changing. My marriage was over, and I had a female who was flirting with me. Could my life be any more complicated? My head was in a mess, and I needed time to work out which direction I wanted to go in. I knew for certain that I no longer wanted to be in my marriage, that was dead, and there was no going back. I felt that John had been given enough chances to change but he had failed to do so. He wasn't too happy that I had announced the marriage was over, but I had to remain strong and stick to my decision to break away from him.

It appeared that he wanted to try and do as much for me as he possibly could that day, which, I knew for certain, was all an act. He offered to cook dinner for me. I found this strange as he had never offered to cook previously. However, I was happy to sort my own meals and I wouldn't be eating with him. I felt that he was starting to panic because he knew he had gone too far the previous night, and he knew I was serious when I had said the marriage was over. He apologised for his behaviour and suggested that we talk. I had nothing more to say on the matter at that point and suggested that we keep out of each other's way. I decided to go for a walk as I needed some air, and to clear my head.

Later that day, John stated that if the marriage was over, he thought it best if one of us moved out. I thought, *Great - I'll get your case!* Obviously, he was annoyed because he didn't get what he was hoping for the previous night, plus I had also refused to have a conversation with him about the state of our marriage. However, he decided that he should be the one to leave and I certainly had no objections.

'I'm sick of keeping up appearances for the benefit of others, John,' I stated.

'I don't see it that way,' was his reply.

'We've been putting on a show in order to please other people for long enough.'

'I'll make arrangements to stay at my mum's.'

'Fine,' I said.

'I'll be out of the house in a couple of days, though I would prefer to stay and sort our marriage out,' he pleaded.

'There's no point, John. There is nothing left within the marriage.'

'I don't want to go,' he declared, with tear-filled eyes.

'We need to make a clean break, so either you go, or I will,' I firmly told him.

'You stay in the house, I'll go,' he suggested.

It was New Year's Day, my marriage had just ended, but I felt such a sense of relief. I had seen a side to John that I didn't want to experience again. I phoned Mum to wish her Happy New Year and arranged to visit the following day. I didn't want to tell her about our marriage over the phone, plus it was New Year's Day, and I didn't want to spoil it for her.

The next day, as promised, I went to see Mum. I disclosed how John had been on New Year's Eve, and revealed the marriage was over.

'That was the final straw, Mum,' I said, with tears

in my eyes. 'He went too far and I'm not willing to put up with that kind of behaviour anymore.'

'He's a fool to himself. He's just thrown everything away,' she replied. When I didn't answer, she asked gently, 'Where is he now?'

'He's at home, packing some of his things.'

We sat in silence for a few moments, then Mum said, 'I've noticed that you've been looking unhappy for some time. I knew he was dragging you down.'

'Do you know what, Mum? I feel better today than I have for a long time because I have finally ended the marriage, which is something I should have done months ago.'

She gave me a big hug and said, 'I think you have made the right decision. You know I'm here for you - always!'

I knew there would be a lot of things that needed to be sorted out between John and I regarding the house. I was hoping that everything could be done amicably. Who was I fooling? I thought I knew John, but his behaviour over the following weeks was, shall I say, less than favourable.

CHAPTER 7

Mixed Emotions

A few days later, Chris phoned. She wanted to know if we would be going to the club on the Saturday evening. 'I can't speak for John, but I won't be going,' I blurted out. Surprised, she asked why. I took a deep breath and revealed that John and I had split up.

'That's no surprise to me,' she declared. 'I knew it was only a matter of time.' She tried to persuade me to go to the club, but I insisted that I just didn't feel up to it. She wondered if I wanted to talk about the break-up, but I didn't feel like doing so at that moment. We chatted for a while. Ending the conversation, Chris said, 'Just get in touch if you need anything.'

I was spending quite a bit of time at Mum's as I didn't like the house and didn't particularly like being there on my own. It probably would have been better if John had stayed in the house and I had been the one to move out, but it had been a mutual decision so that was the situation. The following day, Chris phoned to see if I fancied going out for a coffee. I was happy to, so we arranged a time, and she came and picked me up. We went into town and along with a coffee, she treated me to a light lunch.

I revealed briefly why John and I had split up, but I wasn't prepared to go into too much detail because we were in a public place. I promised to talk to her about it some other time. At that point, Chris said there were other issues that she felt needed talking about which related to New Year's Eve. She wondered if she could call to see me the following day so that we could talk properly. I would be working until 8 pm so I wouldn't be able to see her. I had found a part-time job at a petrol station on the outskirts of town. She offered to pick me up from work, so we could go for a drive and talk in the car. I more than likely wouldn't feel like talking when I had finished work as I would be tired, but she insisted that she would pick me up anyway so I wouldn't have to go home on the bus.

The following evening, she picked me up from work, but I was feeling unwell and wanted to go straight home, have a bath, and go to bed, as I was back at work at 8 am the following morning. She drove me straight home and during the journey I asked her what she was about to tell me on New Year's Eve before John walked in. 'It doesn't matter,' she replied. I pointed out that there was obviously something bothering her, but she said it would keep, and she would tell me some other time.

She was hoping to have a longer chat that evening, but she noticed that I was not in the mood for talking. I had just finished work, I was tired. I wondered if she would mind if we finished the conversation another time when I would be less tired. She didn't mind at all. She dropped me off outside the house, said she would phone me the next day, and then drove off. To be honest, I felt that this short conversation had been a bit of a waste of time.

As promised, Chris phoned me the following day and we chatted for a while. She wanted to call that evening, and I said that I would prefer it if she didn't. She made it clear that we needed to have a proper conversation as a lot of things had been left unsaid. I informed her that I wanted to spend the evening alone. As I had things to do, I was going to be busy all evening and the last thing I needed at that time was a distraction. I was close to Chris, and I knew that there was something bothering her, but I knew she would tell me when she was ready. I wasn't going to put pressure on her.

A couple of days later I was pottering about in the house when John walked in.

'Can we talk?' he asked.

'About what?'

'Our marriage.'

'You were never that keen on talking when we were together, but now we're separated, suddenly you want to talk,' I said, surprised.

'We need to sort this out.'

'There's nothing to sort, John, the marriage is over, and that's final.'

He went into the kitchen and made himself a drink.

'You're out of order, John, thinking you can just walk in whenever it suits you. You're treating the place as though you still live here.'

'Is it a problem, me being here?'

'Not at the moment, but it will be if you turn up on a regular basis.'

'We're making a mistake, splitting up,' he declared.

'We're doing the right thing, John.'

'When did things start to go wrong within the marriage?' he wanted to know.

'When you started being demanding,' I quickly replied.

'I'm sorry if I've ruined things for us.'

'Why have you changed so much?'

'I don't feel that I have,' he replied.

'I would never have married you if you had been like this when we were engaged.'

'Give me the opportunity to change,' he pleaded.

'You've had plenty of opportunities to change but haven't done so,' I pointed out.

'I will change. Things will get better,' he announced, as he walked towards me.

'Do you remember what you uttered at midnight on New Year's Eve?'

'What was that?' he asked.

'A new year, a new start, things will be different,' I reminded him.

'Yes, I do remember,' he replied.

'A few hours after you had made that statement, you acted the way you did when we got home.'

'Do you still love me?' he asked.

'No, John, I don't.'

'What can I do to make you love me?' he wanted to know, as he sat down on the sofa.

'There's nothing you can do now, or in the future, that will make me love you. You've done a lot of irreparable damage within the relationship. I could never love you. The problem with you, John, is you don't like the fact that I won't dance to your tune, and that is when you start kicking off.'

'I'm sorry,' he replied, while rising from the sofa.

'I didn't get married to take orders from you. I would never take orders from anyone within a relationship. I don't believe in giving orders to your partner or taking orders from them. If you had wanted to control someone as soon as you placed a wedding ring on their finger, you picked the wrong person as I won't be controlled by anyone, especially a man.'

'I want to save the marriage,' he uttered.

'It's too little, too late, there's nothing left to save,' was my reply.

The damage had been done, the marriage was over, and as far as I was concerned, he should look upon us as being officially separated. I then informed him that at some point I would be starting divorce proceedings. He finished his coffee, slammed his cup down on the table, and stormed out of the house in a mood - nothing new there! As far as I was concerned, we had officially separated and there was no going back. I felt as though I had been set free!

I needed a break from the house, and everything associated with it. I phoned Mum and asked if I could stay with her, and of course she said that I could. So, I gathered some things together ready for going to Mum's and phoned Chris to tell her that I wouldn't be at home for a couple of days, so there wouldn't be any point in her trying to contact me. I would get in touch with her once I was back from Mum's. I felt that I needed to tell her as I didn't want her phoning or calling at the house and becoming worried when she wasn't getting any response. She sounded disappointed and wondered if there was anything she could do to help. 'There isn't at the moment,' I replied. 'I just need to get out of the house for a few days.'

That evening, Mum and I sat and talked, and I revealed exactly how things had been within my marriage. I had previously mentioned that John and I were struggling with the marriage, and that I was unhappy, but she didn't know the full story. I told her exactly how John had been, and by the end of the evening she knew everything. She gave me a big hug and said that I should have ended the marriage long before I did. She was upset, and now that she knew the full story, she was surprised that we hadn't separated sooner because we had been struggling to keep afloat for a while. In her opinion, I was better off without him.

It had been good talking to Mum, and I felt better as I had got everything off my chest. She was enjoying having me there - it was like old times, but there were things I needed to sort out at home, so it was time for me to return. I arrived back home around lunch time, and within half an hour there was a knock at the door. It was my neighbour. She handed me a bouquet of flowers that had been delivered earlier that day, but as I wasn't at home, the delivery man had left them with her.

She had kept them in water for me so they would remain fresh until I was able to receive them. I thanked her and invited her in for a coffee. She wondered if I was okay and remarked that she hadn't seen John around. She wasn't being nosey; she was a good neighbour and had just wondered if everything was alright. I informed her that John and I had separated and that he had moved out. I disclosed that things weren't working out between us and left it at that. I didn't go into detail of why we had separated, and she didn't ask any further questions. We had a coffee and a nice chat, and she said that if there was anything I needed, just to give her a knock. Once my neighbour had left, I had a proper look at the flowers and the card which came with them. The card read, 'Sorry for everything, I love you.' The flowers were lovely although I wasn't too happy that the sender was John. However, I put them in a vase and placed them on the dining table.

That evening, John phoned. 'Did you receive my flowers?' he wanted to know.

I've been at Mum's, so Claire took them in,' I replied. 'So she saw them before you did,' he retorted.

'Well, obviously,' I replied. There was a silence, so I asked if he was still there.

'The flowers were for you, and I wanted you to be the first person to see them,' he stated, in a raised voice.

'If you're going to be aggressive, John, I will end the call,' I told him. He continued speaking in a hostile manner and I hung up on him, mid-sentence, which felt extremely satisfying!

I phoned Chris to let her know that I was back from Mum's, that I felt in a better frame of mind, and that the break had done me good. She wondered when it would be convenient to call round and see me. I was going to be quite busy doing things in the house, so I said that I would get back to her. A couple of hours later, there was a knock at the door. I had a feeling it would be Chris. I was surprised when I opened the door and saw that it was John.

'What do you want, John?'

'I need some stuff for work,' he replied, gruffly.

'It's strange that you didn't mention it when we were speaking earlier.'

'Well, I would have done if you hadn't hung up on me,' he quickly replied.

'You've got five minutes. Get what you need and go.'

I let him in, and he marched down the hallway and into the lounge.

'Where are the flowers?' he asked.

'On the dining table!' I replied.

He rushed over, snatched the flowers out of the vase, and snapped them in half.

'Why have you done that, John?'

'I wanted you to be the first one to see them, not

her next door!' he replied, angrily.

'Grow up, John! Does it really matter?'

'It does to me,' he quickly replied.

'You go off like this, and then you wonder why our marriage has broken down.'

'I'm sorry, I shouldn't have done that,' he stated, more calmly.

'Why are you sending me flowers anyway?' I wanted to know.

'A man can send his wife flowers, can't he?'

'Of course, but they are normally in love with each other when that happens.'

'You obviously liked them otherwise you wouldn't have put them in a vase.'

'Yes, I did like them. I just didn't like the fact that they were from you.'

'Why didn't you throw them away then?'

'Because unlike you, John, I'm not a waster.'

'I'll arrange for some more to be delivered.'

'I don't want flowers from you, so please don't send any more.'

'I want to send them.'

'Well, send them to someone else, your mum for instance, because I'm not accepting any more flowers from you,' I asserted, in a firm voice.

He said nothing. He just stood there with a vacant expression on his face. I continued, 'Actually, I don't want you to come into this house again for any more things, unless you can guarantee that you'll be respectful and not kick off about something.'

He gathered up the items that he needed and stormed out, once again. Not long after John had left, his mum phoned and asked if she could speak to him. I informed her that he had already left, and as far as I knew, he was on his way back to hers. She went quiet for a moment and then said, 'I didn't know he was coming to mine.'

I said, 'Is he not staying with you?' and she confirmed that he wasn't. I then informed her that we had split up, and apparently, he was supposed to be staying with her. She was surprised as she hadn't seen him. In that case, I didn't know where he was. She wanted to know if I was serious about the break-up, and I declared that I was, and there would be no going back. I was sick and tired of him lying to me and always wanting to be in control.

At that point, she reminded me that she had tried to warn me what he was like before we got married, and I asked her if this was the time when she got to say, 'I told you so.' She stated that she wouldn't do that. I revealed how much John had changed since we got married and emphasised that I wasn't prepared to put up with his lies any longer. I couldn't understand what he was playing at, saying he was going to his mum's and then not arriving, which then made me wonder where he was staying. 'Do you think he's seeing someone else?' she asked tentatively. I said that I wasn't sure, but I wouldn't be surprised. He wasn't staying at his mum's, but he was obviously staying somewhere, with someone. To be honest, I couldn't have cared less if he was seeing someone else, or whose bed he was in, as long as he wasn't in mine. He was away from me, and that's all that mattered.

His mum was sympathetic towards me and stated that she would be having words with John when she finally saw him. She let me know that she was there for me if ever I felt I wanted to have a talk, or if I needed anything.

I was wondering why he had lied about staying with his mum, but then again, this was John, doing what he did best - lying! I could not believe that he had behaved so childishly just because my neighbour had seen the flowers before I had. To me it didn't matter, as I didn't want them in the first place, but to John it had been such a big deal. The way he had carried on made me feel more certain than ever that ending the marriage had been the correct thing to do. We had separated, yet he was still finding ways of getting at me. His behaviour was concerning, and at that moment I felt that I was never going to be free from him. However, this was nothing compared to what ensued over the coming weeks.

CHAPTER 8

A Revelation

I hadn't seen Chris for a while as I had been busy. We had spoken on the phone a couple of times, but she hadn't called at my house. One morning, I was upstairs rearranging things in the wardrobe when I heard a knock at the door. I looked out of the bedroom window and could see Chris's car parked outside. I went downstairs, opened the front door, and she said, 'Hello stranger.'

After inviting her in, I asked if she would like a coffee. 'What brings you here?' I asked breezily as I put the kettle on.

'I was just passing and thought I would call in and see you.'

'I live on a side street, Chris, not a main road - you would hardly be just passing.'

'I was in the area and wanted to check that you were okay. How have you been?'

I sighed and said, 'Not great. My emotions have been all over the place.' I then told her that I was busy sorting wardrobes out. She offered to help me, which was a welcome offer as there was a lot to do. It was one of those jobs that I was wishing I had never started. She also promised to take any unwanted items to the tip if I needed her to at any point.

We ran upstairs, chatting as we went, our footsteps sounding akin to a drum roll. She helped me to completely empty the wardrobe and reposition it at the opposite end of the bedroom. We fell about laughing when we were moving the wardrobe as we couldn't seem to get into the same rhythm. I would be moving it one way, while she would be moving it in the opposite direction. Eventually, we did manage to put it into place, and it was good that she had been there to help me as I wouldn't have managed to move it on my own.

John had left a lot of his things in the main wardrobe, and I wanted to relocate them to the smaller wardrobe in the spare bedroom, so Chris helped me carry all the items through to the other bedroom. This saved me a lot of time, and I was grateful for her help. We were messing about and having a laugh, and it felt good to be letting off a bit of steam. I told her that I was pleased that she had called to see me, seeing as she was 'just passing.' She didn't reply; she just looked at me and smiled. Once we had finished sorting the wardrobes, we went back downstairs, and I suggested that Chris stayed for some lunch. She was happy to.

She wondered if I fancied going for a drive with a view to going for a walk somewhere. It sounded like a good idea, and I was happy to go. Once we had eaten, we drove to a local beauty spot where there was a large grassed open space, and a lake. We parked, got out of the car, and went for a lovely stroll. It was a cool day, but the sun was shining. We were both well wrapped up, and it was nice to be out in the fresh air. After we had been walking for about half an hour, we found a bench beside the lake, where we sat and chatted. It was peaceful, there weren't many people around, so it was the perfect opportunity for us to sit and talk without being overheard.

I told her about the flowers John had sent me and how he had come to the house and destroyed them. I explained how he was still trying to be in control, even though we were no longer living together. She wanted to know why John was sending me flowers when we had separated. I sighed and said he seemed to be under the impression that we would eventually get back together. She wondered if that were a possibility.

'No,' I said categorically. 'As far as I'm concerned, there is no way back for us. I'm going to start divorce proceedings.'

In her opinion, the best thing I could do would be to move out of the house all together and let him move back in. As I didn't like the house anyway, what she had suggested gave me food for thought. I felt that while I was there, John would always keep calling, which is what I didn't want. Plus, the house was depressing me, and I thought that moving out would make me feel a lot happier in myself. I knew that I would be able to move back in with Mum whenever I wanted, so it was something that I was now seriously considering.

Chris reminded me there were other things that we still needed to talk about, and she was hoping they could have been sorted that day. I remained silent while watching the water ripple on the lake as a wild bird passed. I knew there were things that Chris and I needed to discuss, but I was putting it off as I was unsure which way the conversation would go. I enjoyed talking to Chris and spending time with her; she was older than me so she was obviously that little bit wiser. She always seemed to say the right things to lift me up when I was feeling down. We were able to confide in each other, and always felt relaxed when we were together. She commented on how well we got on - she always enjoyed spending time with me and felt that she was able to discuss anything.

Time was getting on and the dusk was descending, so we made our way back to the car and headed for home. I made Chris a coffee when we got back, and we continued chatting. She wondered how I was managing to do my food shopping, and I said I was just buying small amounts on a regular basis in the village. 'I would be more than happy to take you to the big supermarket in town,' she suggested. It was an offer I couldn't resist as there were a lot of things that I needed to stock up on.

When John and I were living together, we always used to do our main shop on a Friday evening after he had finished work. He would come home, have a shower, have his evening meal, and then we would walk up to the small supermarket on the main road of the village where we lived. It was easier then as John would carry most of the shopping bags, but as I was now on my own, I was finding it a bit more difficult. Chris agreed to pick me up from work the following afternoon to take me shopping. After she had left, I sorted my things out for work the next day, had a bath, and went to bed early so that I would feel refreshed the following morning.

As arranged, the following day Chris picked me

up from work and took me to the supermarket. It was nice to have a proper look around the store as that never happened when John and I went shopping. His opinion on shopping was that we made a list, bought only the items on that list, paid for them, and went home. He wouldn't browse or look for offers as he just wanted the shopping trip to be over and done with and for us to get back home as quickly as possible. I hated shopping with him to be honest, but I was enjoying shopping with Chris.

We were taking a nice leisurely walk around the supermarket, which was a different one to where I would normally have shopped. I managed to get stocked up with everything, to the point where I felt that I wouldn't need to do a shop of that size for another three or four weeks. We arrived back home, took the bags in, put the shopping away, and I made Chris a coffee. I then started to chop vegetables for my evening meal and invited Chris to stay and eat with me. It was the least I could do to say thank you for taking me shopping. She accepted with a smile.

It was around 6 pm when we ate and afterwards Chris asked me if I would like her to do the washing up. 'Erm - let me think about that one - go on then!' I replied, laughing. I was starting to feel tired as I didn't feel as though I had had time to unwind since leaving work. 'Would you mind if I went and had a quick shower and got changed while you're washing up?' I asked.

'I don't mind at all. It's your house, you don't need to ask my permission to go and have a shower.'

'I wasn't asking permission, I was asking if you minded, there is a difference. As I've got company, it was polite to ask.'

'Company? It's only me.'

'Well, yes, you've got a point,' was my reply.

'I walked right into that one, didn't I?' was her comeback.

'I won't be too long,' I said, as I walked towards the lounge door.

'Just come here a minute before you go,' Chris requested. I walked into the kitchen and stood beside her at the sink. She scooped up a handful of bubbles and put them on my face. Of course, I couldn't leave it at that, so I felt obliged to do the same to her, and before we knew it there were bubbles all over the place. We needed to stop as I would end up spending all evening cleaning the kitchen, which was not what I had planned on doing.

I went upstairs and had my shower, leaving Chris on pot washing duty, and was back downstairs in less than half an hour, feeling refreshed. Chris had finished the washing up, and she had tidied the kitchen from when we had been messing about with the bubbles. She made herself a coffee and asked me if I wanted one, but I wasn't bothered. I wasn't a huge fan of coffee or tea then, and I'm still not, I can take it or leave it. While Chris was drinking her coffee, we were reminiscing about some of the good times and laughs we used to have in the club. She wondered if I would continue going on a Saturday night, and I said it was unlikely. There was a chance that John might still be going as he was friendly with a few people there, and I didn't want to be drinking anywhere that he was likely to be.

She then suggested that we could go out somewhere different one weekend for a drink if I fancied it. I asked if she and Martin were still going into the club, and she revealed that she wasn't seeing him anymore. I was surprised, as it was the first time she had mentioned it. I wondered if that was her choice or his, and she disclosed that it was her choice because the relationship wasn't going anywhere, and it never would have.

She then revealed that she felt really relaxed, and that she could spend all night talking to me. She also liked the fact that I often came out with something witty, which always amused her. However, I told her I would be kicking her out soon as I had a couple of phone calls to make, plus I didn't want to be too late in bed. I wasn't working the following day, but I wanted to get an early night.

Chris started to gather her things and said that she would go and let me get on with what I had to do. She made her way down the hallway, and we stood talking for a couple of minutes. I thanked her again for taking me shopping and she stated that she would be happy to take me anytime, or anywhere else I needed to go. I gave her a hug and as I was pulling back from the hug, she pulled me towards her and kissed me. It was the most beautiful kiss that I had ever had. It was like something I had never felt before, the kind of kiss that I had always been longing for, the kiss that meant something! Then, reality kicked in and I pulled back from her.

'I can't do this,' I declared, with a panic-stricken face.

'But you just have,' she hastily replied.

I had been lost in the moment and it scared me

'This should not have happened,' I expressed, breathlessly.

'Why?' Chris replied.

'Because I'm not gay.'

'You were enjoying that kiss just as much as I was, so don't fool yourself,' she quickly replied.

'I'm still married for God's sake,' I declared, in a firm voice.

'Married? You're separated! You're getting divorced!'

'This has been a mistake; I want you to leave.'

'We can't leave it like this, things have gone too far,' she insisted.

'Forget what has just happened.'

'I can't.'

'Please just let it go,' I pleaded.

'No, I'm not letting it go,' she persisted.

'Why?'

'Because I'm in love with you, and this is what I've been wanting to tell you.'

'No, this is not happening, this is not what I want,' I declared, walking away from her.

'I think this is exactly what you want,' she replied, with a smile.

'I need to be on my own! Just go, will you please,' I said, unsure how to respond.

'I'll phone you tomorrow.'

'I would prefer it if you didn't,' I retorted.

'Fine, have it your way.'

A loud rattle on the letterbox interrupted my thoughts. *Who the hell is this?* I wondered. I walked past Chris briskly and opened the door. It was John - could my evening get any worse? It seemed that every time I was around Chris, a further situation arose. As I was anxious, he wondered if everything was okay. I told him that things were fine. He then looked at Chris and said, 'What's going on?' She turned, looked at him and said, 'Why don't you ask your wife?' Without another word, she marched out of the house, got in the car, and drove off. I walked back down the hallway and into the lounge. John followed.

'What the hell do you want, John?'

'What was all that about?' he asked, inquisitively.

'We've just had a disagreement about something.'

'Chris seemed rather upset when she left,' he observed.

'It was nothing,' I retorted.

'So, it's gone from being something to nothing.'

'Don't be clever, John! I'm not in the mood,' I told him, categorically.

'So what was it about?' he asked again.

'Leave it, John, it doesn't concern you,' I replied, my voice rising.

'Fine.'

'Why are you here?'

'I need to get my suit as I am going to a function at the weekend.'

'Right, just get it and go.'

'Would you iron me a white shirt?' he enquired, grinning.

'You've got some nerve! No, I will not iron you a shirt.'

'Oh dear, someone has upset you, haven't they?' he uttered in a cocky manner.

'I am sick and tired of you thinking you can turn up here as and when you please.'

'Don't take it out on me because you and Chris have had a disagreement.'

'Right, make arrangements to get all your belongings moved out of this house as soon as possible, and when you've done that, I want your keys.'

'Fine, I'll sort it,' replied John, in an angry voice.

'Make sure you do, and don't turn up here again without phoning first.'

'Are we still meeting in town to go to the bank next Friday?'

'Yes, and make sure you're not late, I'm not hanging about waiting for you.'

'I won't be.'

'Fine, now will you go, please,' I requested, as I opened the door.

He sauntered down the hallway, taking his suit

and un-ironed shirt with him.

I had decided that I was going to bed early that evening, but my emotions were all over the place, so there would have been no point having an early night. I wasn't working the following day so I knew that I could stay in bed a while longer if I was still tired. I sat up until the early hours of the morning, thinking, *What the hell is going on here?* I opened a bottle of wine and poured myself a drink, and one drink led to another, and one thought led to another. I was upset that things had been left the way they had between me and Chris, and I was angry that John had turned up, yet again, without prior warning.

I was close to Chris, but suddenly it felt as though I didn't know her at all. I was questioning myself as to why I hadn't pulled back sooner than I did when she was kissing me, and then realised that I had probably wanted the kiss as much as she did but was too scared to admit it. She had insisted that I was enjoying the kiss as much as she was, and of course she was right. However, that didn't mean that I wanted a full-on relationship with her. I had enjoyed it, but it was as though something just kicked in and made me pull back from her.

I had a drink in my hand and music playing softly in the background. I was listening to a Carpenters record, and the song 'I Need to Be in Love' came on. Listening to the lyrics gave me food for thought. I loved the Carpenters music and knew that Chris did too. I started to regret asking her to leave as it probably would have been better if we had carried on talking and tried to sort things out that evening, but I had panicked. However, I also thought that we both needed to put some distance between us as my head was full of endless questions which only I could answer. She was in love with me, and I just couldn't get my head around that. Something drastically needed to change. If I sat quietly and had a good think about the situation, surely by the end of the evening I would have a clearer vision of what I wanted - or so I thought! I couldn't believe what had happened between me and Chris that evening. This was about as serious as it gets.

CHAPTER 9

Running Scared

On the morning after the night before, I was feeling tired. I hadn't slept much because every time I closed my eyes, I could picture Chris kissing me. I wasn't feeling in the best of moods due to the events of the previous evening. If what had happened between me and Chris wasn't enough, I also had to deal with John after he had turned up unexpectedly - yet again! Also, I knew I had to meet him in town later in the week, which I wasn't looking forward to. I could have stayed in bed as I wasn't working, but my head was all over the place and I couldn't think straight, so I got up early.

I knew that Chris would be phoning me, and although I had told her that I would prefer it if she didn't, I had a feeling that she would still phone. I didn't feel that I wanted to speak to her due to the events of the previous evening, but I could not risk ignoring the phone if it rang in case it was Mum. I knew that Chris and I were close, but I never thought that she would kiss me the way she had done, and I certainly never imagined that she would ever say that she was in love with me.

We had shared a kiss and I had enjoyed it very much; she had ignited something inside me that no one else ever had, and it felt good. However, I had mixed emotions regarding the whole situation and felt that Chris needed to take a step back for the time being.

As promised, Chris phoned and asked me if I was okay. 'Take a wild guess,' was my reply. I didn't want to speak to her at that moment, but she insisted that we needed to talk, as she wasn't happy with the way things had been left. I wasn't happy with what had happened in the first place. She reminded me that we weren't drunk, and that we both knew exactly what we were doing. I stated that people don't have to be drunk in order to do or say things that they later regret. She asked what my feelings were, and I said, 'In relation to what?'

She said, 'Us.'

'As far as I'm concerned, we're close friends and that's it, nothing more.'

'That isn't enough for me, you are all that I think about, I love spending time with you, and I want more than just friendship,' she declared.

I was shocked. My initial reaction was to tell her to back off and give me some space and time to think. She then said, 'I know there is chemistry between us, and if you're honest with yourself, you know that too.' In my mind, I knew there was something special between us, but I had been hurt emotionally within my marriage, and I felt that I was putting up a barrier. I needed to give the situation a lot of serious thought, so I suggested that we kept our distance from each other. I told her that I would get in touch at some point, and we ended the conversation.

I had always been attracted to women, and more so towards women who were a few years older than me, as I always felt that they would be more mature and more experienced, in all areas.

I had never been in a relationship with a woman before. Now that I was faced with the opportunity, I felt out of my depth, and it was scaring me. However, I was questioning myself as to why I didn't just grab this with both hands and go for it, but I had mixed feelings about whether this was the road I wanted to go down. When I had spent the previous evening on my own after Chris had left, I had tried to get things straight in my head, yet I was still having doubts. Yes, we had kissed, and yes, it had meant something to me, but my emotions were still all over the place.

I was twenty-four, and Chris was fourteen years older than me, which didn't bother me in the slightest. I started to question if this was what I really wanted, but I couldn't think straight. I knew what I didn't want, which was a relationship with John, but I felt that I was unable to make any plans. I could sense that Chris was not going to let things drop, and I knew that at some point I would need to have a proper conversation with her. However, I felt that I didn't have the head space for anymore talking at that moment. I would talk to her, but it would be when I felt up to it, and more relaxed.

My life had changed, and I felt that things were moving too fast. Everything around me was falling apart and I was getting to the point where I didn't know what I wanted anymore. I had enjoyed the kiss, but did

I want to take things a step further? It scared me and I was unsure. I thought that the best thing she could have done at that time was to walk away as I wasn't sure whether I would be able to commit fully, but she wouldn't. She was prepared to wait. Then I started to question how I would feel if she did walk away, and that scared me too.

I could not imagine how my life would be without her because we had been friends for several months, and in that time, we had built up a closeness that was special. But did I want to take that to the relationship level? I wasn't sure! A couple of hours passed, and there was a knock at the door. I answered and Chris stood there. I stared at her for a moment.

'Can I come in and talk with you?' she asked.

I sighed and said, 'I feel like you're putting pressure on me. I need to work things out in my own time.'

'Why are you pushing me away?'

'I'm not pushing you away, Chris, I just need time to think.'

'I'm not walking away from this.'

'Why did you leave the way you did last night?'

'Because it seems that whenever I try to get close to you, John appears.'

'Chris, we were kissing! How much closer do you want to get?'

'Did you say anything to him?' Chris wondered.

'Of course not! It's nothing to do with him,' I replied, starting to feel annoyed.

'So, where does this leave things between us?' she asked, taking hold of my hand.

'I don't know, Chris,' I replied, as I let go of her hand and slowly moved away from her.

'When I first met you, I felt that there was a spark from initial eye contact! I don't care how long it takes; I'm not letting you go,' she persisted.

'Your timing is all wrong, Chris; I'm just out of a bad marriage. I've got a lot going on at the moment, and I'm not looking for a new relationship,' I snapped.

'I've waited months to kiss you,' she revealed, giving me a loving smile.

'But it wasn't what I wanted,' I retorted.

'Are you sure about that? Because the way you responded when I started to kiss you, would suggest otherwise,' she stated, with a glint in her eye.

'It was a mistake,' I blurted out.

'Come on, Pauline, you wanted that kiss just as much as I did,' she insisted.

'We need to keep our distance, then see how we both feel.'

'I love you, and I want to be with you,' she revealed, gently placing her hand on my cheek.

'Look, Chris, just give me some breathing space! I need to clear my head.'

'Fine, I'll give you all the space you need.'

'Don't keep phoning me, let things settle down, and I'll be in touch,' I assured her.

'Fine, but just do one thing for me before I leave,' she whispered.

'What's that?' I curiously asked.

'Look me in the eyes and tell me that you haven't got feelings for me, and that you don't want this,' she said, as she moved closer to me.

'No! Just leave it, Chris,' I insisted.

I walked away from her. She followed me, stood in front of me, and took hold of my hand.

'Pauline, look me in the eyes and say it,' she urged.

'I can't,' I blurted out, while desperately trying to avoid eye contact.

'No, I didn't think so,' she said in a soft voice.

'My emotions are all over the place at the moment and I don't need this. Just give me some space - I need time to get my head around all this. You need to appreciate that you have obviously been building up to this for months, whereas it has been a bombshell to me.'

'I realise that.'

'Look, we'll speak soon. I'm sorry, I can't give you an answer right now.'

'Okay, but whichever way this goes, I don't want to lose your friendship,' she stated.

'You won't. We're too close for that to happen,' I assured her.

The conversation ended, Chris kissed me on the cheek, and reluctantly made her way to the door with a look of satisfaction on her face. I smiled and said, 'I'll call you, I promise,' before I closed the door behind her.

A couple of days later, I went into town as I had a few things I needed to sort out, plus I had arranged to meet John. I didn't want to meet him, but I needed to get some money from the bank, and we had a joint account where both signatures were required in order to make a withdrawal. We needed to split the money and open separate accounts because I wasn't prepared to keep meeting him each time I needed money from the bank. Once we had sorted our business out, John asked if he could take me for a drink and some lunch, but I declined.

I explained that the only reason I had met him was to sort things out at the bank. I didn't want to socialise with him. 'But we both used to enjoy going into town for a drink and a meal,' he persisted. I sighed and made it clear that a lot of things had changed since those days. We were no longer together, so we wouldn't be going out together anymore. He didn't respond but looked disappointed. I took the opportunity to point out that he needed to accept the fact that the marriage was over and there was no way back for us. I wanted him to stop phoning me and calling at the house. I turned my back and started to walk away. He shouted, 'Hey, come back!' I felt embarrassed as a few people turned their heads. I turned round and he strode up to me.

'Are you going to tell me what the issue was between you and Chris the other night?'

'Just leave it, John,' I firmly told him.

'I know there is something you're not telling me.'

'You're right - there is something I'm not telling you,' I quickly replied.

'I knew it,' he stated, grinning broadly.

'Do you know why I'm not telling you?'

'No,' he replied, with a bewildered look.

'Because it's none of your bloody business! That's why!'

'You're still my wife,' he quickly replied.

'On paper only,' I retorted.

'We will get back together; I'll make sure of it!'

I rushed away from him as I needed to get on with the other things I had gone into town to do. Once I had finished my shopping, I got on the bus to go back home. I sat upstairs at the front, and as I was waiting for the bus to pull out, I looked through the window and did a double take. It was the type of double take that one of my friends once did when she saw the vodka on offer in the supermarket! (Sorry, I couldn't resist that one, she will be reading this book and she knows who she is.) I had spotted Chris walking on the opposite side of the road. Just seeing her gave me a lovely warm feeling inside and it made me feel good. I wanted to get off the bus to be with her. Then, I noticed that she had stopped outside a shop further down the road and was just standing there as though she was waiting for someone. I was praying that the bus didn't pull out as I wanted to see what she was doing. After a couple of minutes, she was joined by another woman. She looked older than Chris and was dressed in casual clothes. Chris gave her a hug, kissed her on the cheek, and they walked off together.

Immediately I felt envious and found myself thinking, *Who the hell is she?* Or words to that effect.

Then I started to question myself as to why I felt so envious. After all, it wasn't as though we were in a relationship, so it shouldn't have bothered me, but it did. It was at that point that I realised my feelings for Chris were obviously stronger than I had first thought. I knew that Chris and I had agreed to not having any contact for a few days, but I couldn't settle - I needed to know who this woman was, and I needed to know now. However, I could not think of an excuse to get in touch with her. I gave it some thought and decided to phone her, ask if she was okay, and try to bring the subject into the conversation.

During the evening, I phoned Chris and we chatted for a few minutes. She asked me what I'd been up to, and I told her that I had been into town to meet John as there had been things that we needed to sort out at the bank, but I had not done much else. She then revealed that she had been into town to meet her sister for lunch, and she was surprised that we hadn't bumped into each other.

I felt relieved that she had met a member of her family, and I had no reason to disbelieve her as she had volunteered that information herself; I didn't have to ask her. I did eventually meet her sister and knew that Chris had been honest with me. I promised that I would call her in a couple of days' time, when I would hopefully be able to make a decision.

That evening Mum phoned.

'John's been in touch,' she informed me

'Has he been to your house?'

'No, he phoned me.'

'What did he want?' I was eager to know.

'He wants me to try and persuade you to take him back!'

'I'm not taking him back, Mum!'

'I reminded him that he's been a fool and thrown everything away,' she revealed.

'What was his reply to that?'

'He hung up on me.'

I was annoyed that he had been bothering Mum. I intended having a word with him about it at some point. I just could not get through to John; he would not accept the fact that the marriage was over.

CHAPTER 10

Decision Time

D ays went on and Chris and I had no contact with each other. Not seeing her was difficult because we were close friends, who were getting so much closer. However, I did want to have some much-needed thinking time as I had an important decision to make, and I could not afford to make the wrong choice. In that time, I did a lot more thinking and tried to put things into perspective. I thought about the kiss we had shared, and how I felt each time I was around her, and it made me feel good. Also, the fact that I had been so envious when I had seen her in town with another female made me look at the situation differently. If I hadn't been attracted to her, I wouldn't have cared less who she had been meeting in town, so for me, that said it all. The way I had reacted told me everything I needed to know about my feelings for her, and I was now starting to look at Chris in a completely different way.

All the thoughts in my head were of her, and every thought gave me a warm feeling inside. I needed to stop fighting these feelings and admit to myself that I was most definitely gay, and was very much attracted to her. I decided to phone her, and we had a nice long chat. After she asked if she could come down that evening, I revealed that I was going to Mum's. She then went quiet, and I wanted to know what was wrong. She admitted she had been hoping to see me because things had been left a bit awkward between us, and we did need to sit down and talk things through, properly!

She confided her true feelings - she needed to see me as she was missing me. She felt that we had spent enough time apart, and that we needed to sort things out, one way or the other. I was more than happy to sit and talk, but I had already arranged to visit Mum, so I didn't want to cancel our arrangement as we were both looking forward to it. Chris understood but also said, 'I can't seem to get my timing right with anything at the moment.'

She wondered how long I was going to Mum's for, and I informed her that I would only be there overnight and would be back home the following day. She was welcome to come down when I was back home if she was free, and we could talk. She wondered if I would like to go out for a meal the following evening, and I told her I would love to. We arranged for her to pick me up at 6 pm.

After I put the phone down, I started to get my things together, ready for going to Mum's. Time was getting on, and I knew that she was cooking an evening meal for us, so I didn't want to be late. I called in town on my way to Mum's as I wanted to get her some flowers. Whenever I visited, I always took her flowers or chocolates, as she loved both. I arrived at her house and was met with the lovely aroma of a roast dinner, which soon got my taste buds tingling. She was a good cook, and I was looking forward to tucking into my meal. She had also been baking, which she often did when she knew I was visiting. She had made two apple pies, a custard tart, and a fruit cake. I didn't like fruit cake; she had made that for herself, but I was certainly looking forward to getting stuck into the apple pie. Her apple pie was to die for, and I knew that she would be putting one of the pies in a container for me to take home, which she always did.

We finished our meal, then had a stroll to the local pub for a couple of drinks. I loved spending time with Mum. We always got on so well and we both had a good sense of humour. I can never remember being in Mum's company and us not laughing about something. I had always been able to talk to Mum about anything, we were so close, but I just couldn't bring myself to tell her what had been happening between me and Chris. I felt that I needed to make a firm decision, on my own, before sharing the news with anyone, including Mum. I had a pretty good idea which way things would be going with me and Chris, but I knew that telling Mum would be one of the hardest things I had ever had to do.

I stayed the night at Mum's, and the following day we went into our local town as she needed to do some shopping. We had a good browse around the shops, and I took her for a light lunch. I didn't want to eat anything too heavy as I knew that Chris and I were going out for a meal in the evening, so I didn't want to spoil my appetite. A couple of hours later, we went back to Mum's, and we chatted for a while. I revealed that I was going out for a meal that evening with Chris. I had spoken to

Mum about Chris in the past, but they had never met. She knew that she was a close friend and that we used to meet up for a drink on Saturday evenings. I stayed with Mum for around an hour, and then started to gather my things together ready for going back home as I knew that Chris would be picking me up at 6 pm. While I was doing so, Mum was packaging the apple pie to take with me. I thanked her for a lovely evening and a lovely day and left to make my way home.

When I got home, I had a quick shower and put away the few things I had bought that day. Chris arrived at 5:45 pm and came into the house for a few minutes while I finished getting ready. She gave me a box of chocolates which was a nice surprise. I thanked her and kissed her on the cheek.

She told me that I looked lovely and then asked me where I would like to go to eat. I was happy to leave the choice up to her. We got in the car, and she suggested a nice pub that she had been to in the past with family. We were chatting while she was driving, and she said that we needed to sit down and talk things through. I agreed with her and stated that I was happy to do so once we were back home. We had a delicious meal and arrived back home around 9 pm. I made Chris a coffee and we had a long chat. I disclosed exactly why my marriage had ended, and that there was no going back for me and John. She had always known that John and I weren't getting on well but was hoping that we didn't stop going out on a Saturday evening.

She then stated that the relationship between her and Martin would never have worked, for obvious reasons. She revealed that she hadn't been seeing him that long, and it was just friendship between them. She had only continued going out at the weekend with him in order to see me. She wanted to know why I had ever got married, as it was obvious that I was gay by the way I had initially responded to her kiss. Getting married had been the biggest mistake I had ever made, and doubts had plagued me, even on the morning of my wedding day. I revealed that yes, I was attracted to women, but I thought that I was probably trying to ignore my feelings and getting married seemed the right thing to do, at the time. She wondered whether I would have stayed with John if he hadn't changed so much after we got married. I confirmed that it was very unlikely because I was obviously gay, and at some point, I feel that the right woman would have come along, and I would have ended it with John.

'The right woman has come along,' she declared.

'I know, but my marriage hasn't ended because of you. My marriage has ended because of the way John has been conducting himself for the last eighteen months.' I referred to New Year's Eve and how I wasn't too sure at first whether I would be going out. She said that it would have ruined her evening if I hadn't gone. She got a lovely warm feeling inside when she saw me that night, as it was all that she had been wanting all day.

I asked her why she had been flirting with me on New Year's Eve and for a few weeks before that. She revealed that she had had feelings for me for a while, and flirting was her way of getting closer to me. She didn't think that it had been that obvious. I pointed out to her that I had suspected it for a while, and I was surprised that John hadn't noticed. She thought he may have noticed but just not said anything. I was pretty sure that he would have had something to say to either me or her, if he had noticed. It was unlikely that he would have kept his opinions to himself.

She then said, 'Anyway, if you suspected that I was flirting with you, how come you didn't say anything to me about it at the time?'

'I almost did at one point but wondered whether I had misread the situation. If I had questioned you about it and you had denied it, I would have felt embarrassed. I could have got things so wrong, and it could have cost me the friendship, which was something I didn't want to risk.' I revealed.

She had noticed that John seemed to be quite clingy on New Year's Eve and that she couldn't seem to get time on her own with me. I explained that things weren't that good between me and John at that time, and that it seemed as though he was putting on a show that evening to make it appear that things were good between us. Chris said, 'Well, he didn't fool me.' She revealed how envious she felt when John kissed me at midnight, but she was unable to do anything about it. I then confided how much I didn't want him to kiss me, and how much I was dreading the hour approaching. I reminded her that she had kissed me on the cheek, so she got her kiss after all.

'Do you think that's all I wanted, a kiss on the cheek?'

'At the time, yes, but I now know different,' I replied.

'You are all that I think about, and I want so much for us to be together.'

'I know you do; you have made that obvious.'

'Does being in a relationship with another woman scare you?' she wanted to know.

'Slightly, as I have never been in a relationship with a woman before, and it's the fear of entering unknown territory.'

'Neither have I, so we would be entering it together.'

'Chris, I know you so well, I am attracted to you, and I couldn't think of anyone else I would rather be in a relationship with.'

'So what are you saying?'

'Let's do this,' I whispered, looking into her eyes.

'Are you sure?' she replied, with a loving smile.

'Yes! I want to be with you,' I declared.

'Do you know how good it makes me feel to hear you say that?'

'Do you know something, Chris? This is a conversation that I could never have envisaged you and I having.'

'Me neither, as I never thought I would ever stand a chance with you,' she replied.

'It's good that we've talked things through properly instead of rushing into anything.'

'Oh, I don't think anyone could accuse us of rushing into it! It's taken a while for us to have this conversation.'

'Finally, things are moving in the right direction,' I said, smiling at her.

'I would have waited, no matter how long it took.'

'You really are in love with me, aren't you?' I remarked.

'Very much,' she replied, while giving me a beautiful smile.

We had talked things through properly and the evening had flown. It was getting late, and I needed to go to bed as I was at work the following morning, then I had a few days off. As we stood in the hallway, I thanked Chris for a lovely evening. It had been good to see her, and I was confident that we could make a go of things. A smile lit up her face. I knew that Chris was in love with me because I could see it in her eyes. She said I was special to her, and being with me was something she had wanted more than anything, for a long time.

She wondered when she could see me again. 'Why not come round tomorrow evening at 7 pm and I'll make us something to eat?' I suggested. 'If that's okay with you,' I added, a little hesitantly.

'That would be wonderful,' she agreed, smiling.

A more serious look appeared on her face, and she asked if she could kiss me, without being thrown out, which was what had more or less happened when she had kissed me properly for the first time. I replied, 'Go ahead.' She put her arms around me, gave me a beautiful kiss and promised she would see me the following evening. 'See you tomorrow,' I said, cheerfully, as I closed the door behind her.

After she had left, I sat quietly collecting my thoughts. We had done a lot of talking, and I felt that the evening had gone well. I had enjoyed being with her. Each time we were together, a lovely warm feeling welled up inside me. I loved everything about her. I loved the way she looked at me, the way she made me feel, and the way her eyes lit up when I walked into the room. She had obviously spent a lot more time thinking things through than I had, as she was in love with me long before I knew.

However, I appreciated the fact that she had been so patient with me. She had given me time to sort my head out in order to make the correct decision. I wanted a relationship with her, and I felt that it was time for things to start moving forward between us. We had said that this was going to be something new for both of us, therefore we had decided to take things slowly. I was now feeling much better emotionally, and I knew that she was right for me. She was a part of my life, she was special to me, and I now knew that she was the one that I wanted to be with.

CHAPTER 11

A New Relationship

The first thing I thought about when I woke up was Chris, and it gave me a lovely feeling inside. I was up bright and early for work. I was happy, and everything felt good. I was looking forward to cooking a meal that evening and spending time with her, though I was hoping and praying that this wouldn't be one of the nights when John took it upon himself to come to the house. He still had his keys, and although he often knocked at the door, he had also been known to let himself in, which I didn't want to happen, especially tonight. I needed to get his keys off him - there was no real reason why he still needed to have a set. On my way home from work, I called in town and got a couple of bottles of wine as I felt that it would be nice to have a drink with our meal, and afterwards. I also decided to buy a couple of bolts for the doors because I knew I would feel happier if John wouldn't be able to walk in.

While I was in town, I bumped into John's mum. It was lovely to see her as I hadn't seen her since John and I had separated. She greeted me with a big hug and said I was looking well. We went for a coffee and a chat, and she disclosed that John was now staying with her, though she hadn't managed to find out where he had previously been staying. He wouldn't share that information with her. I asked her if he was behaving himself, and she admitted that she hadn't seen that much of him because when he wasn't working, he was out drinking. She was concerned about me and wondered if I was coping on my own. Smiling, I reassured her that I was fine, and I felt better than I had in a long time. It had been great seeing her, but time was getting on, and I needed to make my way home. Chris would be arriving at 7 pm and there were things I needed to do before she arrived.

When I got home, I started to prepare the food for the evening and realised that Chris wouldn't be able to have a drink as she was driving. It didn't matter - I knew the wine I had bought would come in handy for another evening. I was playing music, and a lot of the songs related to how I was feeling. They were feelings of happiness and excitement. I couldn't get thoughts of Chris out of my mind; I was thinking about her constantly. She had taken over my head, and the more I didn't see her, the more I wanted her to be there with me. These were feelings that I had never felt for anyone else. I had certainly never had feelings like this for John. I couldn't fight it and realised what was happening to me - I was falling in love with her! Not only had I been with the wrong choice of partner, but I had also been with a partner of the wrong gender. I was now in a much better place and realised that I wanted things to work between us. I now knew what love was, and all the feelings that went with it. I had fallen for her. She was all I could think of, and I wanted so much to hold her and feel her close to me.

Once everything had been prepared for dinner, I had a shower and got changed. As her arrival time became closer, I was filled with a mixture of nervousness and excitement. I had only seen her the previous evening, but I was missing her. When the knock came at the door, you would have thought that I was a fourteen-year-old going on a first date. My heart was beating like a drum, and I had a lovely warm feeling inside. I thought to myself, *What is wrong with you? Just get a grip.* I had never felt anything like this when I went on my first date with John, or any other guy for that matter. So, for me, that said it all. This was my first date with a female, and it was the best feeling ever. I composed myself and went to open the door, trying to appear all calm and collected. She would never have guessed that I had been pacing the floor five minutes before she arrived.

Chris said she had missed me. As she looked at me, I could see that her eyes were full of love. I had missed her too, and it was good to see her. She then gave me a beautiful kiss and handed me a bottle of white wine. I pointed out that she wouldn't be able to drink as she was driving. The wine was for me, she said. She would have coffee. I went into the kitchen to pour myself a glass of wine, and while I did so, Chris was standing in the doorway looking at me. As I was pouring the wine, she came up behind me and put her arms around my waist. She made me jump; it was awful ... I ended up knocking the glass of wine over! I turned around to get a cloth and she pulled me towards her, and I kissed her. It was so passionate, and at that moment I could not have cared less if anyone had walked into the room - I don't think we would have stopped.

I mentioned that I had bought a couple of bolts for the doors and was hoping to fit them before she arrived but hadn't had time. She offered to fit them; I was delighted as it would save me a job. I gave her the necessary tools, and she made a start. She wondered why I was putting bolts on the doors, and I disclosed that John had been known to let himself in, and I didn't want him doing so and ruining the evening for us. I didn't particularly like having bolts on the doors, but they were utilitarian, and I felt so much happier knowing that there was now no chance of us having an unwelcome visitor. Plus, as I was now living on my own, they would be added security. After we had eaten, I poured another glass of wine and we sat and talked. Everything that we had been wanting to say to each other finally came out that evening.

'Are you sure that you definitely want this?' Chris asked.

'More than anything,' I replied, while gazing into her eyes.

'So, what's changed your mind about us? That evening when I first kissed you in the hallway, you couldn't get me out of the house fast enough.'

'I couldn't get that first kiss out of my mind, and the more I didn't see you, the more I wanted to,' I admitted, smiling at her.

I appreciated the fact that she had given me time to think because I had a decision to make which would change my whole life completely. I had to be sure. She revealed that she had been clock watching all day as she couldn't wait for the time to arrive when she would be able to see me, but she had also felt slightly nervous about the evening. She then wondered if I had felt nervous. 'No, not at all,' was my reply. I smiled at her and revealed that I had been pacing the floor before she arrived.

She reminded me how much she had enjoyed our first kiss that we had shared weeks ago. She knew she was taking a risk in kissing me, but it was a risk that she was prepared to take. She couldn't believe it when I suddenly pulled back, as she could tell that I was enjoying it as much as she was. I was enjoying it, up to a certain point, but then, for some reason, reality kicked in and I panicked. Chris said, 'You do realise that the relationship is going to attract a lot of problems.' I assured her that we would work through them together, and that we would both need to be strong. After all, this was the 1980s and gay relationships were still frowned upon.

She asked me what I thought my mum would say when I told her that I was in a relationship with a woman. I wasn't sure but hoped that she would be okay about it. 'What about John, how do you think he will react?' she wondered.

'I couldn't care less what he has to say! It's none of his business. Being with him is a part of my life that I want to erase,' was my reply. 'At some point, I will start divorce proceedings as I need to sever all ties with him, and get him out of my life for good.'

'How do you think your sister will react when you tell her about us?' I was eager to know.

'I don't think she will take the news too well,' she said with a sigh.

'Will that bother you?'

'Of course it will, but it's not going to change anything. It's my life, we're together now, and I won't allow anyone to come between us.'

She looked into my eyes and said, 'I love you and will always be there for you.'

I had a hospital appointment the following day in Sheffield, and Chris offered to take me. She suggested going into the town centre for some lunch and a look around the shops after my appointment. It sounded like a great idea, and I was looking forward to spending the day with her. Mum would normally have come with me, but on this occasion, she had a prior engagement which she couldn't cancel, so I was happy that Chris had offered to come. She said that she would like to be back home for around 6 pm as she was going to visit her sister for a couple of hours, if I didn't mind. I was happy for her to go and wondered if it was something that she did every week. She revealed that it was something they had done for years. 'You need to continue doing the things that you did before we got together,' I assured her.

It was getting late, so we decided to call it a night as we had to be up early the following morning for my hospital appointment. Chris left around 11pm after we had arranged for her to pick me up at 9 am for my 10:45 am appointment.

The following morning, Chris arrived at 8:30 am. 'You're early,' I said with a smile as I opened the door.

'Well, I wouldn't mind a quick coffee before we leave,' she suggested. I made her a drink, which she sipped while I finished getting ready. We set off just after 9 am. We wanted to give ourselves plenty of time to get there as the traffic was likely to be busy at that time in the morning.

Following my appointment, we went into Sheffield town centre for some lunch. Later, we had a lovely afternoon browsing around the shops. I wanted a couple of new tops, so I was dragging Chris around quite a few shops, and she was more than happy for us to do that. She would have to get used to long shopping trips as it normally took me ages to make a choice! She then mentioned that she had noticed it takes me a while to make my mind up about things, tongue in cheek. I did eventually find two tops that I particularly liked and tried them on. I asked Chris for her opinion. She liked them both and offered to pay for one of them.

It was the first time that we had been shopping, apart from food shopping, and we were enjoying our time together; she was spoiling me. We arrived back home at 5:30 pm and Chris came in for a coffee but didn't stay long as she was going to see her sister. I thanked her for a lovely afternoon, she finished her coffee, promised she would phone me later, and left.

I phoned Mum to let her know how I had gone on at the hospital. I revealed that Chris had taken me, and we had had a lovely afternoon in Sheffield. She said it was good that Chris had been able to go to the hospital with me. She would like to meet her.

Later that evening, Chris phoned to say that she had enjoyed spending the day with me, and she couldn't wait to see me again. I told her that I was going to Mum's the following day as I was doing some painting for her and would probably be staying a couple of nights. I wanted to make sure that the painting was finished before returning home. She sounded disappointed. 'That means I'm not going to see you for two or three days. I'm going to miss you so much.'

'I'll phone you from Mum's in the evening and we can have a nice chat,' I suggested.

'Will you be telling your mum about us?'

'No, it's too soon,' I stated.

This was a complete lifestyle change for both of us. I thought we needed more time to get used to the relationship ourselves before telling anyone, and Chris agreed. We finished our conversation, I got everything ready for going to Mum's the following day and then went to bed. I was up at 7 am the following morning as I wanted to set off early to get started with the painting. I knew that Mum had gone into town for a couple of hours, so I just let myself in and got started.

Mum came back from town around lunchtime, bringing me a couple of my favourite treats, which made me smile. I don't think it matters how old a daughter or son is, your mum will always buy your favourite things when she knows you are visiting. I painted until around 3:30 pm, and then I had to stop as the light was fading and I didn't like painting in artificial light. That was the only drawback with decorating in winter, by mid-afternoon you had lost the light.

The following day, I managed to get the painting finished, therefore I could have gone back home that evening, but I decided to stay for the second night, as planned. In the evening I asked Mum if she minded if I phoned Chris. She didn't mind at all. It was polite to ask, as it was her phone, and she paid the bill. I knew that I would be able to talk privately with Chris because Mum would be in the lounge with the TV on, and I would be on the phone in the hallway, although I knew that Mum wouldn't be listening anyway; she wasn't like that.

I had a nice conversation with Chris and let her know I would be back home the following day. She was eager to see me. I would probably arrive home at around 3 pm, so I asked her if she wanted to call in the evening for a drink. 'I would love us both to have a proper drink, but you know I can't drink when I'm driving,' she said. I didn't respond. 'I could always stay over,' she suggested.

'We'll see how the evening goes,' was all I could say.

We ended the conversation, and I went back into the lounge. Mum was engrossed in the TV.

Mum poured us both a drink, turned the sound down on the TV, and we chatted. She asked how Chris was, and I told her that she was fine and that she would be calling the following evening for a drink. 'You seem to be spending a lot of time with her,' Mum commented.

'We're good friends, we get on well, and we enjoy each other's company,' I replied. I thought to myself, *Oh God, I'm sure Mum is starting to suspect something.* It would have been the ideal time to tell her about me and Chris, but I just couldn't tell her at that point. The relationship was new to us, and we wanted to adjust to it ourselves before telling Mum, or anyone else. It would keep for another time. I changed the subject and we talked about other things. At around 10 pm, I started to feel tired, so I decided to go to bed, and Mum stayed up for a while watching TV.

The following morning, I was up bright and early and made breakfast for both of us. I stayed with Mum until just after lunch, then got my things together ready for leaving. It had been lovely spending a couple of days with Mum, as it always was. She walked to the bus stop with me and as the bus was approaching, she gave me a hug and a kiss and said, 'Enjoy your evening with Chris.'

I called in town as I wanted to buy some more drinks for us to have that evening, plus I wanted to get something for Chris. I knew that she liked dark chocolates, so I wanted to get a box to give to her that evening. I was looking forward to seeing her. I had missed her and couldn't wait for 7 pm to arrive.

CHAPTER 12

A Night to Remember

I arrived back home from Mum's around 4 pm and put away the things I had bought in town. I had eaten at Mum's, so I didn't need to cook anything when I got home. I had plenty of food in the fridge if we wanted a sandwich during the evening. I felt in a good mood as I knew it wouldn't be long before I would be seeing Chris. I had a shower and put on the new top Chris had bought for me in Sheffield. I poured myself a glass of wine, put some music on, and waited for her to arrive.

I was thinking about our new relationship, and how Chris made me feel. She was caring, loving, attractive, and sexy. She ticked all the right boxes. She was everything I wanted, and when we were together, I just couldn't keep my eyes off her. I started to wonder why it had taken me so long to make my mind up about having a relationship with her, but I needed to be 100% certain before I made the commitment. Chris and I were close, but I never anticipated that we would ever form a relationship. Never in my wildest dreams could I ever have imagined that I would have fallen in love with a woman eighteen months after my wedding day. This was real, it was happening, and it was the best feeling ever.

At 7 pm I heard a knock at the door. It was Chris, and I just couldn't wait for her to come in so I could put my arms around her and kiss her. I had missed her so much and it was good to see her and hold her close to me. As soon as I had got the other set of keys from John, I would give them to her, then she would be able to let herself in whenever she wanted. I asked her what she wanted to drink, and she told me that she would like a glass of wine. While I was pouring the wine, she commented on my new top. She said I looked lovely.

I gave her the glass of wine, and the chocolates, which she thanked me for, and said they would more than likely be opened before the end of the evening. We were chatting, and I reminded her about the hug she had given me in the hallway when John and I were still together, and how she had taken a chance as he was only in the lounge. She revealed how good being close to me had made her feel, and that she couldn't let go. I confessed I had gone to bed that night wondering what the hell was going on and why she was flirting with me.

'I had wanted to be with you for a long time,' she admitted, 'but I never thought it would ever happen, although I could see that things weren't good within your marriage.'

'Yes, things were terrible between me and John,' I agreed.

'You would not believe how many times I had wanted to kiss you but didn't want to chance it and risk losing you as a friend. I came so close to kissing you on New Year's Eve, when we were talking in the kitchen, but then John walked in,' she revealed.

'I wouldn't have allowed it to happen as John and I were still together,' I disclosed.

'Your marriage was a sham; you were on the verge of breaking up.'

'I know,' I replied, 'but we were still together, and I don't believe in messing about with someone else when you're in a relationship, even if that relationship is bad. Do the right thing, end it, and move on.'

'I was about to tell you I had feelings for you that night, so when he walked in, I was fuming,' she confessed.

'I feel that he arrived at exactly the right time,' I said, voicing my opinion.

She then admitted that once John and I had separated, she couldn't hold back any longer and just decided to go for it and kiss me. I was curious to know when she became aware of her feelings for me. She revealed it was just friendship initially, but then her feelings started to get stronger, and she was unable to stop thinking about me. She explained how she felt envious if John showed me any affection and started to feel resentment towards him. I asked her why.

'Because he was the one that was sitting close to you, he was the one that could kiss you whenever he wanted, and he was the one who would be sleeping with you when you got home.'

'I can assure you, there was nothing happening in the bedroom department, and hadn't been for some time,' I confided.

She confessed that she hated seeing us together but knew that she had to tolerate John to see me. I wanted to know what she was initially attracted to, and she told me that she loved my personality, my sense of humour, the way I dressed, and my eyes. It appeared that both Chris and I were attracted to the beauty of a person's eyes. To be honest, it's one of the first things I notice on a person.

I also detect whether a woman is wearing a wedding ring, which incidentally proves nothing. Don't assume that a woman isn't gay because she has a ring on her finger. I was wearing a wedding ring, but it didn't stop me falling in love with a woman. Chris had also been married, but that didn't stop her falling in love with me. Appearances can be deceptive; you can be married and still be attracted to someone of the same sex.

We were listening to music, and two songs could have been written for us. One song was 'All of My Life' by Diana Ross, and the other was 'Suddenly' by Cliff Richard and Olivia Newton John. The lyrics summed up everything that was happening between us, and we always looked upon them as being 'our songs.' I think in every relationship there is always that one song that is significant. I enjoyed listening to music, and suddenly all the songs were about us. I took hold of her hand and pulled her towards me, and we danced slowly. She kissed me and whispered, 'I'm so in love with you.'

I replied without hesitation, 'I'm in love with you too.'

At that point, Chris pulled back from me and looked into my eyes. I asked her what was wrong, and she said, 'Those are words that I never thought I would ever hear. This is all I have ever wanted.' We were in such a good place that night, and I knew that the feelings we had were mutual. It was a lovely evening, and we felt so relaxed, we had so much respect for each other, and I thought this is exactly how things should feel in a relationship.

The drinks were flowing, one drink led to several, which led to Chris not being able to drive home. Tentatively, she asked if she could stay the night. She was welcome to stay, and I said that I would make up the spare bed. She quickly turned her head and looked at me with a surprised expression. I just smiled at her, winked, and said, 'You think I'm joking!' The look on her face was priceless, but she didn't question it or put me under any pressure. I wasn't used to this because she was treating me exactly how I expect to be treated. At that point I knew everything was going to work out fine between us. She didn't want to leave as the evening had been so lovely and she didn't want it to end. If I hadn't allowed her to stay, she would have got a taxi home, but I wanted her to stay. We had both known she would be driving, yet we continued to pour drinks. To be honest, I had a feeling that the evening had been planned to go that way, on both sides.

I went upstairs and made up the bed in the spare room, while Chris poured us another drink. I knew that Chris wanted us to sleep together, her eyes and her body language had been telling me all evening, and yes, it was what I wanted too. Very often, if you concentrate on a person's eyes, they will tell you more than words could ever say, and Chris's eyes had been undressing me all evening. I study a person's eyes when I am talking to them. I can get lost in them, especially if they have beautiful eyes. I loved her, and although I was nervous, I wanted us to spend the night together. However, I wasn't prepared to sleep with her in the bed where John and I had slept when we were still together, which is why I made up the bed in the spare room.

When I came back to the lounge, we were talking and one of the questions I asked Chris was why it had taken her so long to get around to saying what she had wanted to say to me on New Year's Eve. She declared that the moment had felt right on that evening, but John had ruined it by walking in on us. She had been plucking up courage to say it since things had gone pear-shaped on New Year's Eve, but she couldn't seem to find the right opportunity. I told her that I knew she had had something on her mind, and I also knew that she would tell me in her own time. I then added, 'Although I could never have imagined that you were going to say you were in love with me.'

'I felt compelled to tell you when we had kissed in the hallway that evening as I couldn't keep it bottled up any longer,' she admitted. Although I had pulled back from her, she had felt that the moment was right to say how she was feeling.

We were cuddled up on the sofa with the music playing low in the background, and she looked into my eyes and said, 'I love you so much.' She had made that obvious by the way she had been looking at me all evening. I felt so close to her, and relaxed, and right at that moment there was nowhere else I would have wanted to be. I felt so happy being with her, she made me feel special, and I knew that I had made the correct decision to be with her. It had been a lovely evening, but it was getting late. We finished our drinks and went to bed.

I was up first the following morning and just sat quietly with a drink waiting for Chris to get up. I felt as though everything that I had ever dreamed of had happened the previous evening. It made me realise why being with John had felt so wrong, and it confirmed that I had never been in love with him. This was a partnership based on mutual respect and I loved her so much. Everything in the relationship felt right. I felt alive, I was happy, life was good! I had entered into a new relationship with a woman I was crazy about. Although it was a touch scary, it was a lovely feeling.

As I was gazing out of the window, I heard Chris coming into the lounge. She stood behind me and kissed my neck. It was lovely to feel her warm lips caressing me. I went into the kitchen to make her a coffee, and she stood in the doorway, leaning on the door frame. I could sense that she was staring at me, so I turned and smiled at her. She winked at me and said, 'Is everything okay?'

I walked towards her, kissed her, and said, 'Perfect.' We both had showers and cooked breakfast together. We were on a real high and nothing could have burst the bubble we were in. We had shared a magical evening - which I wanted to last forever. We were so much in love. This was the real thing, and we were both so happy.

We decided to go for a walk mid-morning, as Chris was unable to drive due to drinking the previous evening. We spent a couple of hours strolling in the park, then went back home, and I made Chris a coffee. In the afternoon, we put the TV on to watch a film.

We were both lying on the sofa, and Chris was running her fingers through my hair, which was relaxing. Consequently, we both fell asleep and missed most of the film.

We had something to eat early evening, which I was prepared to make, but Chris offered to cook. I didn't object - it was nice to have someone other than Mum cooking a meal for me, as I normally did the cooking when I was with John. I don't think it ever occurred to him that I might have liked a meal cooked for me.

Chris and I had spent a lovely day together, and we had talked about such a lot of things relating to our future. She wondered if I would like her to stay over again that night. I revealed that I would, but it was probably better if she didn't as I needed to get an early night. I was going to Mum's to help her with some jobs in the house, so I didn't want to be too tired when I arrived. I wasn't staying over at Mum's - I wanted to be back home around teatime as I had some writing to catch up with. I would have liked Chris to stay the night, but I was tired, and I had pre-arranged things to do the following day, so I needed to get a good night's sleep. I knew that if she stayed, we would end up having another late night. She understood, and it was lovely not to feel pressured in any way. I knew that things were going to work out long term for us. She was giving me everything I had always longed for in a relationship.

She went home around 8 pm and I spent the remainder of the evening alone. I reminisced about the previous night and played the two songs which had meant so much to us. I was missing her like crazy. She phoned and said she couldn't get me out of her mind; she was unable to concentrate on anything. I had the same feeling. She mentioned a song she wanted me to listen to, and then said she loved me. 'Love you too,' I replied.

After our conversation, I went and put the song straight on. It was called, 'I Won't Last a Day Without You' by the Carpenters. It was beautiful, in fact it made me cry! I was in a new relationship with someone who cared about me, and it felt great. She was the one I had been searching for all along, and we had so much respect for each other. She made my heart race, and I wanted to spend as much time with her as possible. I was happy and it was lovely to be with someone who didn't kick off if they didn't get their own way.

We were so gentle and loving towards each other, and it was a relationship that was completely different from any other relationship I had been in. It was certainly different from the relationship John and I had. The feelings I had when I was with her were feelings that I had never felt for anyone else. It felt right, and I knew that, at last, I was on the correct path.

However, we both had to adjust to this new life we were entering, and the task of telling family and friends lay ahead of us. I was very close to Mum, and I could tell her anything, but this would be the hardest thing that I had ever had to tell her. If my marriage being over wasn't bad enough, I then had to tell Mum that I was in a relationship with another woman.

We knew it would be a difficult journey, but it was a journey we would be making together, and I knew that the love we had for each other would get us through anything. Things were exciting, as they often are at the start of a new relationship. We had both found what we had been searching for, and were looking forward to making plans and starting a new life together.

Little did we know that it would become a roller-coaster of a ride!

CHAPTER 13

Things Turn Nasty

A few days passed and the relationship was going great. Chris and I were so happy. I knew that I would miss her today. I wasn't seeing her as we both had pre-arranged things to do. I went to Mum's early and helped her with some jobs, and then we went into town for lunch. I arrived back home from Mum's mid-afternoon. I intended to get several things done without any distractions.

I had been back home a couple of hours when the phone rang. It was John, wanting to know if it was okay to call that evening to collect some more of his things. I informed him that it wasn't convenient as I was busy, but he insisted there were things that he needed. I said, 'Fine, in that case you had better come and get what you need, but I want you straight in and out.' I was hoping to get some more writing done, but it was now looking unlikely. An hour later he arrived, and I knew straight away that he had been drinking. He wasn't drunk, but I could tell that he had had quite a bit to drink. He sauntered in.

'I'm seeing more of you now than I did when we were living together,' I remarked.

'I've taken the day off work and been out for a few drinks.'

'Evidently,' I expressed.

'I could do with something to eat. You wouldn't make me a sandwich, would you?'

'You're right, I wouldn't,' I retorted. 'It's not a café.'

He pushed past me and rushed into the kitchen. I followed him. He opened the fridge and took some food out.

'What do you think you're doing?'

'Half of the food in this house is mine,' he claimed.

'Grow up, John, do you think I haven't done any shopping since you left?'

I went to pour myself a glass of wine. He asked me if I was okay, and I said that I was fine. He wanted to know if I had seen much of Chris, and I stated that she had been here a few nights before. He asked if we had had a nice evening, and I confirmed that we had. He wondered what Chris and I had been doing all evening.

'Why all the questions?'

'I'm just showing an interest and making conversation,' he replied.

'We chatted over a drink, had some food, and listened to music.'

'Food that I've paid for,' he retorted.

I pointed out to him I had bought all the food that was now in the house. He wanted to know what time

Chris had gone home, and I revealed that she had ended up staying the night due to having too much to drink and being unable to drive home.

'She could have got a taxi.'

'She could have, but she didn't. Have you got a problem with that?' I was starting to feel irritated now.

I didn't need to tell him that Chris had stayed the night, but I decided to, because if I hadn't, the nosey neighbour next door certainly would have. She would have noticed that Chris's car had been parked outside overnight, because she missed nothing, and she would have gone out of her way to question John about it if she had seen him. He asked me if I would get him a beer from the fridge and I refused. He had had enough to drink. I didn't want him to have any more.

'What have you come here for, John?'

'I've already told you; I need some more things.'

'Well, hurry up, get your things, and go.'

I enquired about how his mum was, and he claimed he hadn't seen much of her, which I could appreciate as he would be at work during the day, and in the pub every evening. I didn't let on that I knew he had been staying elsewhere, because there would be repercussions if he were to find out that his mum had shared that information with me. To be honest, I couldn't have cared less where he was staying. He was out of the marital home and that was all that mattered to me.

While taking a sip of my drink, I noticed he was looking at me in a strange way. Suddenly he uttered, 'Did you sleep with her?' That was one question I certainly wasn't prepared for; I nearly dropped my glass. I thought, *Get a grip, woman, you can't be spilling wine again!* I just looked at him, turned around, and walked out of the kitchen, without answering. I thought to myself, *Where's Chris when I need her?* I carried on walking into the living room, and he followed me.

'I'm not doing this, John; I'm not going to be interrogated.' I hoped that I sounded firm. I didn't want my tone of voice to give anything away.

'I've seen the way she looks at you,' he alleged, with a smirk on his face.

'And what way might that be?'

'Seductive glances. She couldn't take her eyes off you.'

'Ha! You wouldn't recognise a seductive glance if it smacked you in the face.'

'Don't be clever,' he snapped.

'And don't you come in here questioning me.' I was now getting annoyed with him.

'Why won't you just admit that you slept with her?' he wanted to know.

'My personal life has got nothing more to do with you,' I hastily retorted.

'Can I stay over?'

'No!' I replied, in a firm voice.

'You let *her* stay over though, didn't you?' he taunted.

'Because she had been drinking and couldn't drive,' I explained.

'I've been drinking.'

'Grow up, John! You're not driving, and if you were, you still wouldn't be staying.'

'I want to make love to you,' he disclosed, as he slowly walked over towards me.

'What you mean is that you want to have sex with me. You've not made love to me since we got married,' I replied, as I stepped away from him.

'What do you mean?'

'There was no passion, John. We didn't make love, it was just sex, there is a difference! I never wanted to sleep with you when we were living together, and I'm certainly not going to now.'

'I found it passionate,' he insisted.

'Sorry, but I didn't,' I replied.

'It doesn't have to be this way.'

'It does, John, you've had a drink and you've come here tonight for one reason only, but it's not happening,' I firmly told him.

'I bet you didn't say "No" to Chris last night.'

I paused, as I went to pour another drink. I was unsure how to reply.

'No, I didn't,' I eventually revealed.

'I'm lost for words! I knew it! So, you did sleep together,' he said, smugly.

'Well, that didn't take you long, did it?'

'What's that?'

'To find those words that were lost.'

'Don't be sarcastic,' he replied.

'Will you go, please?' I urged.

'Did you enjoy sex with her?'

'I'm not discussing it with you or anyone else.'

'Was sex with a woman better than with me?' he was keen to know.

'Have you heard yourself? You don't even come close, mate! Put it this way, I would never sleep with a man again, ever! Does that answer your question?'

'Were you and her together before we split up?' he asked, curiously.

'No! So don't even think of going down that road.'

The argument ended and he started to gather his things together. I wanted his keys before he left, and he stated he wasn't giving them to me. He had thrown his teddy out of the pram because he hadn't got what he had hoped to get. I told him in no uncertain terms that I didn't want him coming to the house anymore.

He informed me that while there were things of his in the house, he would be coming round. I then re-minded him that I had previously told him to remove all his things from the house. I wanted him to take all his belongings as I wasn't prepared to go through this again. The next time he came to the house would be his last visit.

I asked him why he disrespected women the way he did, but he wouldn't answer. 'What's the matter, John, is the truth getting to you?' I asked. He had no respect for me, and no respect for his mother. He was stomping around and banging about. 'Look at you now, because you haven't got your own way. You're a married man and yet you're acting like a child.'

He banged his keys down on the table and shouted, 'There's my keys.' I went to pick them up and he reached over and picked them back up before I could grab them - I rest my case!

'You're so childish, John. Keep the keys! I'll change the locks.'

Then, because I had suggested that he kept the keys, he threw them in my direction. He marched down the hallway towards the front door, but I didn't hear the door open. Suddenly he appeared back in the lounge and stated that he wanted to apologise for his behaviour.

'Well, go on then.'

'I'm sorry.'

'Now get out.'

He sat on the sofa and said he knew he had been out of order and that it wouldn't happen again.

'Yes, but it has happened again. You were sorry last time, and the time before that, yet it keeps happening over and over again. The trouble with you, John, is, if you're not getting what you want, when you want it, you're spitting your dummy out!' So, the argument started again!

Round Two!

'Why did you sleep with her?' he probed, his voice rising.

'I don't have to justify myself to you or anyone else.'

'End it with her,' he insisted.

'You can't handle the fact that I'm sleeping with a woman, and not you.'

'You were never interested in sleeping with me.'

'What does that tell you? It proves how different things can be when you're with the right partner.'

'Does your mum know?' he asked, smirking.

'Not yet, and don't you even think of telling her,' I insisted, staring at him.

'I thought you loved me.'

'You destroyed any feelings that I had for you! You put a wedding ring on my finger, and you completely changed.'

'Don't you want to save our marriage?'

'No, I don't! I've had enough of being in a relationship where I feel pressured.'

'I'll change,' he promised, as he started to get emotional.

'No, you won't! I'm sick of your constant lies, and the sulking if things don't go your way. If you were going to change, you would have already done so.'

'I'm sorry,' he professed, with tears in his eyes.

'I don't love you, John, and I don't want the marriage. We agreed that we were separated - yet here you are.'

'What is so special about Chris?'

'Where would you like me to start? She's got respect! She's kind, considerate, affectionate and she makes me feel special, which is something you never did. In fact, she's everything that you're not,' I pointed out to him.

'You and Chris won't last; I'll destroy you,' he stated, strutting out of the lounge.

'Oh, one last thing,' I shouted, as he headed off down the hallway - again!

'What's that?'

'Don't forget to bang the door on your way out,' I said, relieved to see him go.

As soon as he had gone, I locked the door. I didn't want him walking back in. I had hoped that we could have remained on reasonable terms, but his behaviour that evening had ruined that. From now on, I felt that I could only be civil with him while we dealt with issues relating to the house. I was upset and angry, and what I wanted most of all was for Chris to be there and hug me. I poured myself another drink, which I desperately needed, and sat quietly, thinking about how nasty John had been.

Around 8:30 pm, the phone started ringing, but I ignored it. A couple of minutes later it rang again, at which point I decided to answer it. It was Chris, saying that she needed to speak to me urgently. I wondered what the problem was, but she declined to say over the phone and informed me that she was coming to see me. I started to wonder if she was having second thoughts about our relationship, but then realised it was unlikely. Thoughts were filling my head as I tried to work out what could possibly be wrong.

About half an hour later, Chris arrived. I could

tell by the look on her face that she was both annoyed and upset. She stood in front of me, held my hands and kissed me. She put her arms around me and hugged me tight. She didn't want to let go.

'What's wrong?' I asked.

'I've had a phone call from John.'

'What did he want?'

'He said that you have agreed to get back together, and he's moving back in,' she tearfully revealed.

'Chris, there is no way I would ever take John back, you know that,' I assured her.

'Has he been here tonight?' she was keen to know.

'Yes, he came to get some things, and we argued.'

'How does he know about our relationship?'

'He guessed, and I couldn't see any point in denying it,' I revealed.

'What was his response?'

'He said he will destroy us,' I replied with tears in my eyes.

'Sweetheart, no one will ever destroy us,' she assured me.

'He's so convinced that me and him will get back together.'

'Well, apparently, I've seduced you and broken his marriage up.'

'He's the one who broke the marriage up, due to his behaviour,' I quickly replied.

'He knew that we had slept together and insisted

that I keep my hands to myself and stay away from you. He was abrupt on the phone.'

'I'm sorry that you've had to endure that behaviour from him,' I said, as I put my arms around her.

'I wasn't going to be dictated to, which is why I ended the conversation with him,' she replied.

'Good for you,' I uttered, smiling at her.

'I knew he was lying, and that you would never get back together. I just needed to hear it from you.'

I reassured her that I didn't want anyone else. I would certainly never get back with John, and he knew that, he just wouldn't accept it! She wondered what game he was playing, and I revealed that he had come round in the hope of staying the night, but it had backfired, and he was now trying to cause trouble between us. This was his way of getting back at me. I was upset at the way John had been, and I was annoyed that he had phoned Chris and upset her too. 'I'll stay the night,' she whispered. This was music to my ears as I wanted her to be with me. I poured her a vodka and lime, and I had a gin. It was a change from wine, and to be honest, I didn't seem to be having much luck with wine, I was spilling more than I was drinking.

We discussed everything that had happened that night, how John had behaved, and how angry and upset he had made us feel. She couldn't believe it when she answered the phone, and it was John. She thought he sounded drunk, which didn't surprise me. He must have had some more to drink prior to phoning her. I knew exactly how John's mind worked. He knew that he had been out of order that night, and that things were over between us. He was looking for someone to blame, and that someone was going to be Chris. She should ignore anything that he said to her as this was what he did to people. The trouble with John was that he always knew he was doing wrong, yet he kept on doing it, and it always got to the point where he felt guilty, couldn't handle it, and tried to blame the situation on other people. I needed to break away from him all together, and everything associated with him, and felt that my only option was to move out of the house.

I was pleased that Chris had called as I was missing her. Everything was okay now, she was here with me, and that was all I wanted.

CHAPTER 14

Back Home with Mum

T he following morning, I was up and showered early. I had things to do which I hadn't managed to finish the previous evening due to John calling. I left Chris in bed as I knew she had had a bad night; she was restless and at one point she had gone downstairs to make herself a drink. When I asked her what was wrong, she advised me to go back to sleep.

I went downstairs, made myself a drink, and did the writing I had been hoping to finish the previous evening. I had kept a diary for many years. I had quite a bit to catch up on, and I wanted to do as much as possible before Chris emerged. As she hadn't slept well, I decided to leave her in bed until around 10 am as I knew she wouldn't want to be in bed any later than that. However, she sauntered into the lounge at 9:30 am. I closed my book and said I would finish the writing later in the day, when she had gone home, but she persuaded me to continue. I carried on for a while but then stopped as Chris was too much of a distraction, a lovely distraction I hasten to add. She was constantly looking at me, and I couldn't concentrate.

'Why couldn't you sleep last night?' I asked.

'I'm worried about you.'

'Why?'

'Because of how John is with you.'

'Don't worry about me. I can handle John,' I assured her.

'Why didn't you leave him sooner?' she wondered.

'You just hope that things will change.'

'What was he like before you were married?'

'He was a completely different person. We had our ups and downs, as you do, but we always sorted things out,' I revealed.

Sometimes the relationship was on, then it was off, but there always seemed to be something that drew us back together. But once we got married everything changed, and I think he was under the impression that it was his God-given right to be in control. If that was the case, he married the wrong person because I wouldn't be controlled, not by him, or anyone else. I don't know what went wrong, but it was as though he completely changed towards women in general. He started to be offhand with his mum, and at times, with my mum. It was as though he had had a personality change.

He was totally different before we got married, otherwise I would never have married him, but once he placed the ring on my finger, things went downhill. He could be kind and loving, when it suited him, but also controlling. This is why, along with obvious other reasons, the marriage would never have worked as I don't take orders from anyone within a relationship, and certainly not from a man! I thought I loved him but now I knew it wasn't love. I turned to Chris and confided, 'I have only realised what love is since getting involved with you.' She looked at me and smiled. 'You make me so happy, and I love having you in my life,' I whispered.

She assured me that she would never do anything to hurt me, and she knew that I would never hurt her. She wondered if John had ever hit me, and I confirmed that he hadn't. He wouldn't dare because I would have reported it immediately. He was never violent within the relationship, but he was controlling in other ways. This was still affecting me emotionally and I needed to break away from everything associated with him.

Chris went to have a shower, and I took the opportunity to get more writing done. When she came back downstairs, I made us both something to eat. Neither of us had eaten breakfast so we decided to have an early lunch and then go for a walk. I knew that Chris would be leaving around 1 pm as she had an appointment at 2:30 pm and needed to go back home first. While we were having lunch, Chris wondered if I still intended moving out of the house. I nodded. It was something I needed to do. I no longer felt comfortable there because it was a place where John had made me feel so unhappy and was continuing to do so. While I remained in the house, John would keep finding excuses to call, so I needed to sever all ties with the property and get away to make a fresh start. I mentioned that I would have a word with Mum with a view to moving back home.

She then said, 'Move in with me.'

'I would love to at some point, but not yet, it's too soon,' I hastily replied. I was rather shocked at her invitation, as we hadn't been together that long.

I decided to ask Mum if I could move back in, and Chris offered to drop me off at Mum's on her way home. Chris explained that, although we wouldn't be able to see as much of each other, she thought I was making the right decision. After lunch, we went for a short walk and before we knew it, it was 1 pm and time for Chris to leave. Standing in the hallway, I gave her a set of keys. She would now be able to let herself in, instead of knocking each time she came round, although hopefully I wouldn't be living there much longer.

While I was at Mum's, I told her about the visit from John the previous evening and how he had been with me. I expressed how much I wanted to move out of the house. I felt that I could no longer live there, because he was turning up as and when it suited him. I didn't need to ask if I could move back in with her; she made the offer herself. 'Get your things packed up, get out of the house, and move back home,' she insisted.

She wondered if Chris would help to move some of my things in her car, and I was sure she would be happy to help. The larger items would be moved by one of Mum's friends, as he had access to a van. I knew that moving would mean Chris and I wouldn't be able to spend as much time together, but for my own peace of mind, it was what I needed to do, and Chris agreed.

I phoned John at work and informed him that I was moving out of the house. Somewhat reluctantly, I said I needed to see him that evening so that we could discuss things. He arranged to call after work which

would be around 6:30 pm. When he arrived, he apologised again for his behaviour the previous evening. I
didn't want to discuss it. I pointed out that he was lucky
to be back in the house. Since I was moving in with
Mum, he might as well move back in. He wondered why
I was moving, and I revealed that I was sick of him turning up. He suggested that I stay in the house, and that he
wouldn't turn up again. I confirmed that I was moving
out, it had all been arranged, and that was final.

We discussed how we were going to divide items
up within the property. I wrote down everything that
we had agreed, which we both signed, and each had a
copy. I didn't trust John. I wanted to make sure that
everything we had agreed was put down in writing and
signed. That way, he couldn't say that I had taken things
out of the house that we hadn't agreed on. I informed
him that it would be a few days before I was packed up
and ready to leave, and that I didn't want him coming to
the house again while I was still there. I would let him
know once I had moved out, and I would leave the keys
with my neighbour for him to collect. It was then up to
him when he moved back in.

I felt that the meeting with him had gone better
than I had expected. For the first time since we had separated, John had been amiable. I asked him why things
couldn't have been like this when he had called in the
past. He then said, 'If you're referring to last night, it
was because I had been drinking, and I apologise.' I had
lost count of how many times he had had to apologise
for his behaviour in the past due to drink. However,
everything that was relevant had been sorted, so I was
satisfied. I informed him that as soon as I moved out of

the house, I would be putting in for a divorce.

Once John had left, I phoned Mum and Chris to let them know how the meeting with him had gone. I wasn't seeing Chris that evening, as I was working the following morning and needed to get to bed early. However, she had offered to pick me up the next day after work and help me do some packing. I needed to get all my personal belongings out of the house as I didn't trust John. If I were to leave things there, he would probably have destroyed them after he moved in.

The following day, we packed as much stuff as we could into Chris's car and drove to Mum's. It was the first time they had met, and I introduced her as a friend because I hadn't told Mum that Chris and I were together. They seemed to get on well, and Chris revealed that she liked Mum. We made quite a few trips over a few days as there were a lot of things to transport, but finally everything was sorted. I was on my way back home to Mum's. Mixed emotions swirled around as I locked the door to the house for the last time. It was a place where John had made me feel unhappy. It was also the place where Chris and I had spent our first night together, which was so special. However, it was time to move on.

Chris was visiting her sister in the evening, so I would spend time with Mum. It had been a busy day; I was tired and just wanted to relax. I poured drinks for us, and we chatted. She asked me what John's mum thought of us splitting up, and I revealed that she was there for me if I needed her. No doubt John would have given her a completely different version of events from what had actually happened, but then again, she knew her son and knew how much of a liar he was. We both got on well with John's mum; he wouldn't fool her, just as he was unable to fool me. She always claimed that she loved having me as a daughter-in-law, and I always loved visiting her.

I needed to tell Mum about me and Chris and felt that it was the ideal opportunity. My mum was very broadminded and easy-going, but I did have misgivings of how she would take the news. Parental disapproval sticks with you, so I needed Mum to be okay about our relationship. I poured us both another drink and decided to just go for it and tell her.

'What do you think to Chris, now you've met her?'

'I like her, she's nice,' Mum replied.

'Mum, there's something I need to tell you,' I could hardly get my words out.

'What's that?'

'It's about me and Chris,' I began.

'Go on,' she said, smiling at me.

She had a look on her face that said, 'I know exactly what you're going to say.'

'We're more than just friends,' I revealed, as I struggled to get the words out.

'I was wondering when you were going to tell me.'

'You knew?'

'Of course I knew, I'm your mother! All the signs were there.'

'In what way?'

'The amount of time you've been spending with

her. I was watching you both while she's been helping you to move back in here. The way you look at each other, and the way you are when you're together. My suspicions were confirmed.'

'How do you feel about it?'

'Sweetheart, it makes no difference to me, as long as you are happy.'

'Mum, I couldn't be happier, and I'm so much in love with her.'

'If you're happy, I'm happy! I haven't got a problem with it,' she assured me.

'We're so good together, Mum. She's everything I ever wanted in a relationship, and we want to start a new life together.'

'And I will support you, every step of the way.'

I felt relieved now that it was out in the open and I thanked Mum for being so understanding. We thought that we had been keeping things low-key, but Chris and I couldn't help but look at each other in a certain way when we were together; our eyes just wouldn't let us hide the feelings we had for each other. Our body language had given it away, and Mum had obviously picked up on it. Your mum always knows. You may be able to fool other people, but you can never fool your mum.

She knew that I had not been happy for a while and was pleased that Chris was bringing some happiness back into my life. She wanted to know if John was aware of our relationship. I informed her that he was, and he planned to split us up. She pointed out that if we loved each other so much, there was no way that John would be able to split us up, which of course was true! She gave me a big hug and stated that I looked happier and more relaxed than I had for months. It didn't matter to her whether I was in a relationship with a male or a female. All she wanted was for me to be happy. I was so relieved that everything had gone well, as things always seem that much better when you have your mum's approval.

The following week, Mum invited Chris for Sunday lunch. Things seemed a little awkward at first in the way that no one seemed to know what to say, but it was short-lived, as Mum soon got a conversation going. They got on well - I was relieved! I couldn't have cared less what anyone else thought; we had Mum's approval, and that was all I needed.

I used to see Chris most nights. She would pick me up, and we would go out in the car and just drive for miles, park up somewhere, and sit and talk or listen to music. Mum always said that we didn't need to keep going out in the evening as we were welcome to spend time at hers. On one occasion, Mum let me know she was going out for the evening with a friend and suggested that Chris and I might as well stay in the house rather than going out for a drive. Chris enjoyed driving and was happy for us to go out in the evening. Mum pointed out that we would have the house to ourselves for a few hours, tongue in cheek! I told her that I would see what Chris wanted to do.

The evening arrived, and we decided to stay at Mum's, obviously! Chris came to Mum's around 5 pm, because we were having a meal with Mum before she went out. Mum's taxi arrived at 7 pm, and I went to the door with her. As she was leaving, she pointed out that she had booked a return taxi for 10 pm. She smiled and whispered, 'Make the most of it.'

She returned home at 10:15 pm, and Chris left around 11 pm. I went out to the car with Chris, and she suddenly realised that she didn't have her watch. I asked when she last had it, and she said she was wearing it when she arrived at Mum's. 'In that case, it must be somewhere in the house,' I replied. Suddenly, it dawned on her that she had taken it off and placed it on the drawers at the side of the bed.

'Oh, bloody hell, Chris.'

'I know - just shoot me now,' she replied. I promised to find it and give it to her the following day. She drove off, and I went back into the house. I went straight upstairs, and the watch was exactly where Chris had stated, so I just popped it into the drawer.

I went back downstairs, and Mum wanted to know if Chris and I had had a good night. I confirmed that we had. 'I thought you had when I saw Chris's watch on the drawers,' she said.

'Oh, right, well this is a bit awkward,' I replied. I thought, *There could have only been one thing worse than this, and that would have been if she had come home early.* She said that as long as we had had a good night, that was all that mattered. She had seen the watch when she had gone to hang her clothes in the wardrobe, as it was situated in my room. I requested that she didn't say anything to Chris, and she assured me that she wouldn't.

The following day, Chris came to pick me up, and we went into town. She wondered if I had her watch, and I took it out of my bag and gave it to her. She hoped Mum hadn't seen the watch at the side of the bed, at which point I went quiet. She asked if Mum had seen it, and I admitted that she had. I wouldn't have voluntarily shared that information with her, but as she had probed, I wasn't going to lie to her. 'Well, that's just great!' she said. I reassured her that everything was fine, and that Mum wouldn't say anything to her. I did point out to Chris that Mum had indicated that we made the most of the time we had on our own in the house while she was out for the evening.

I was enjoying being at Mum's. It was good to be back home with her and she had invited Chris to call anytime. However, Chris and I were a couple, and we weren't having enough quality time together. After a few weeks, Chris asked me again to move in with her as she was eager for us to start living together. I was settled at Mum's, and it would mean that I would be packing up and moving once again. However, we wanted to spend more time together, so I decided to move in with her. This meant that we could at last start living like a proper couple. I was starting a new life with Chris, I loved her so much and we were both looking forward to the journey we would be making. As far as we were both concerned, it was onwards and upwards.

CHAPTER 15

A Step Too Far

I had moved out of Mum's and in with Chris. It took a bit of time to get used to living together, but things were going great, and we were enjoying spending more time with each other. We would still visit Mum on a regular basis, or she would come to us, and very often stay for a meal. I was pleased that Mum and Chris were getting on well, it meant a lot to me. We were so happy and looking forward to everything that life had to offer. However, I feel that whenever you are at your happiest, there is always someone who wants to take that away from you. Sure enough this was the case, in the form of John.

We were watching TV one evening when the phone rang. Chris answered it and it was John. He stated that he needed to speak to me urgently, so Chris shouted me into the hallway. I asked him what he wanted, and he informed me that he would like to meet as there were things he wanted to discuss in private.

'I'm not going to meet you,' I asserted.

'I've got nothing left.'

'And who's fault is that?'

'I still love you,' he declared.

I made it clear that I didn't want to continue talking and I ended the conversation. I went back into the lounge, and Chris was eager to know what John wanted.

'Apparently he has something he needs to talk to me about in private,' I said.

'Like what?' she asked. I stated that I had no idea, and I wasn't interested. Things were left at that, and we carried on with the evening. I poured us both a drink, and we continued watching TV.

About an hour later, there was a knock at the door, and Chris and I just looked at each other. We weren't expecting anyone. I said, 'Surely not.'

'It had better not be him!' exclaimed Chris. He knew where Chris lived as he had worked on her car outside the house when we were still together. She went to the door, and sure enough, it was John. She asked him what the hell he was doing here, and he informed her that he wanted to speak to his wife, in private. She shouted to me, asking if I wanted to speak to him, and I said that I didn't. I heard him say that he wasn't leaving until he had spoken to me. At that point, Chris closed the door on him and came back into the lounge.

'I don't believe this! I moved out of the house to get away from him, and now he's turned up here,' I remarked, my voice rising. He knocked on the door again. This time I answered it and said, 'You've got five minutes, John.' He wanted to come into the house, but I insisted that we talked on the doorstep or not at all.

He revealed that he was still in love with me, he wanted me to take him back, and he didn't want a divorce. He claimed he wasn't coping living without me. I reminded him that I wasn't coping when I was living with him. He stated that he knew he had done wrong, and he wanted the chance to prove that he had changed. In my opinion, he had had all the chances he was getting, he needed to accept that we were finished, and there was no going back. 'I've got a new partner, we're happy, and it's not going to change,' I concluded.

At that point, Chris appeared in the hallway and said, 'Right, John, I'm going to tell you this, and I'll tell you once only, if you contact either of us in any way again, I will personally get in touch with the police.' She revealed that she had a relative in the force, which was true, and that she would contact them for advice if John bothered us again. She then told him to go.

Apparently, he couldn't go because he had lost a contact lens and needed to find it. He asked me if I would help him to look for it, and Chris closed the door on him. If he had lost it, then it needed to be found. His eyesight was poor, so he wouldn't be able to find it on his own. I informed Chris that I would help him look for it, and she marched off back into the lounge. It was dark, so I went to get a torch to search for the lens, locking the door behind me as I didn't trust him. I had lost count of how many hours we had spent searching for lost contact lenses in the past. We once searched part of a pub car park because he had lost one.

'Thanks for helping me,' he uttered.

'You had better not be messing me about, John, saying that you have lost it when you haven't,' I warned. 'Maybe you should dispense with the contact lenses once and for all and revert to wearing glasses.'

'Knowing my luck, the lens would fall out of the frame,' he quipped.

We both started laughing. 'That would just be the sort of thing that would happen to you.'

'I miss this,' he stated.

'What, crawling around looking for lost contact lenses?'

'No, us talking properly and laughing.'

'Well, you had it all and threw it away.'

'I know the marriage broke down because of my behaviour. I'm so sorry.'

Eventually I found the lens, he thanked me and leaned towards me to give me a kiss. I said, 'No, John.'

He wanted me to give him one last chance to put things right, and I informed him that he had run out of chances and that we would never get back together. He needed to accept that I wasn't in love with him, and that I was in a new relationship.

I requested that he didn't phone or turn up at the door again and reminded him what Chris had said. I pointed out that he didn't need to make things more difficult than they already were. 'I know, and I'm sorry,' he replied. He then told me to look after myself and reminded me that he would always be there if I needed him. He turned, sauntered towards the gate, and left.

I went back into the lounge and Chris looked furious.

'What's wrong?'

'Nothing,' she replied.

'Oh, I think there is!' I went to pour a drink and asked her if she wanted one, but she didn't answer.

'Was that a yes, a no, or have you got the face on?' I quipped. She didn't respond. 'We need to talk,' I went on.

'I've got nothing to say,' she snapped.

'Come on, this is silly, just tell me what's wrong.'

'Well, actually …' she began, which wasn't good. It always concerns me when you ask someone what's wrong, and their reply starts with, 'Well, actually.' However, things were frosty between us, so it needed sorting out.

'What's the problem?'

'You and him,' she replied.

'What do you mean?'

'You and John, laughing and joking outside.'

'Oh, for God's sake, Chris, he happened to say something funny.'

'And of course, you had to laugh,' she replied, sarcastically.

'Well, that's what people normally do when they hear something funny. As you know, I've got a good sense of humour and I laugh at things that are funny. I sometimes even laugh at things that other people don't find funny. You need to get used to that.'

'You seemed to have plenty to say to each other,' she observed.

'We were just making general conversation,' I pointed out to her.

'Did you find the contact lens?' she asked.

'Yes.'

'What have you got to do to get through to him?' she wondered, longing for a solution.

'He will eventually get tired of playing games and leave us alone,' I affirmed.

'He's putting pressure on our relationship that I can't handle,' was her reply.

'So what are you saying?' I asked, as I moved closer to her.

'I'm not sure.'

'Don't mess me about, Chris! If you've got something to say, let's hear it.'

'Fine! I feel that he's coming between us.'

'And that's exactly what he wants! He knows if he persists, it will get to us.'

'It appears to be getting to me more than it's getting to you - why?'

'Because I know him. He will eventually get fed up with it all,' I assured her.

'Why haven't you put in for a divorce yet?' she questioned, in a firm voice.

'Because there have been so many other things to sort out,' I quickly replied.

'He wants you back,' she stated.

'I'm not going back - and you know that' was my reply.

'You're still married. You could go back to him at

any time,' she alleged.

'I could - but I'm not going to,' I stated, unsure of how else to convince her.

'I've waited a long time for this relationship. I'm not going to lose you.'

'Listen to me, you're not going to lose me,' I assured her.

'Can you guarantee that?' she asked, while looking into my eyes.

'Yes! Chris we're living together, how much more commitment do you want?'

'I love you so much,' she declared.

'And I love you, which is why we'll get through this,' I assured her.

'I'm so sorry, he's really got to me tonight,' she stated, while taking hold of my hand.

'Considering you had nothing to say, you've not done bad,' I quipped.

I reassured her that I was confident we would not hear any more from John. She revealed that she was sick of him trying to spoil things for us. I walked over to her, and she put her arms around me and hugged me. 'I'm sorry, he's getting to me,' she whispered.

'He is trying to cause trouble between us, and he is succeeding,' I began; 'Look at us tonight, you're letting him win, and he would get a real kick out of it if he thought he was making things uncomfortable for us.' We had had our first argument, although it was more of a heated discussion than a full-blown argument. He would have been delighted if he had known he had caused trouble between us. I suggested that she put him out of her mind and just enjoy the rest of the evening.

I poured us both a drink and put some music on to help us wind down as it had been an emotional evening. I reminded her that we knew from the start that our relationship would not be easy and that we would run into problems. She remarked that John was the only one causing problems for us, which was true. I put my arms around her, kissed her, and we slow danced to one of the songs that was playing. I told her that I loved her more than anything, and that I was so pleased that she had been persistent in the beginning. 'I'm in love with you, and I wasn't prepared to back off,' she reminded me.

The following day, we went to Mum's and let her know what had happened the previous evening. She was disgusted at John's behaviour and advised us to remain strong and ignore him, which was easier said than done. In the afternoon, Chris had an appointment in town, so she left after about half an hour, but I stayed at Mum's. We talked, and Mum asked if things were okay between me and Chris, and I said that John was putting a lot of pressure on the relationship. Tears trickled down my cheeks as I told Mum that I didn't want to lose Chris, and she assured me that I wouldn't. I wondered how she could be so certain.

'I don't think you realise just how much Chris loves you. She worships the ground you walk on.'

'I know she does, Mum, and I love her so much.'

She reminded me that she liked Chris and was

pleased that I had finally found someone who was making me happy and treating me with respect.

She wondered if I had spoken to John's mum, and I confirmed that I hadn't spoken to her recently. She was a lovely lady and Mum got on well with her, they were good friends. She lived in a large house with a business attached, and Mum used to clean for her once a week. She was good to Mum as not only did she pay her for cleaning, but she also used to take Mum out occasionally for lunch. I used to love visiting her. John and I used to go for tea every Sunday when we were together, and she always put on a nice spread. I enjoyed spending time with her, we used to make each other laugh, and I was missing seeing her. I felt that things needed to settle down between me and John before I contacted her again.

At that point, the door opened and in walked Chris. She smiled at me and winked. She had a box of chocolates in her hand which she gave to Mum to say 'thank you' for supporting us. Mum thanked her, gave her a hug and said, 'As long as my lass is happy, that's all that matters to me.' I made us all a drink, we spent another hour at Mum's, and then left.

While driving, Chris suggested that we went for a meal.

'What's the reason?' I asked.

'Do I need a reason to take my girlfriend out for a meal?'

'It wouldn't be because it's your turn to cook, would it?' I quipped.

She just smiled at me.

I told Chris it was a nice gesture to buy the chocolates for Mum. She expressed that Mum had been supportive from the start and that she appreciated it so much. Mum was the best, and I knew she would be there to support us every step of the way. She was a pretty good judge of character, and she had stated from the start that she liked Chris. Chris said it was a pity that everyone wasn't like Mum.

We talked that evening and made a few plans for our future. When I informed Chris that I was going to contact a solicitor to start divorce proceedings, she turned her head, looked at me and gave me a lovely smile. I warned her that John would not be happy that I was putting in for a divorce, and that I was expecting trouble from him. She reassured me that I shouldn't have to deal with John once the solicitor had been appointed as they would do the corresponding. I dreaded to think what his reaction would be when he received a letter from my solicitor, but there was no going back. I wanted to get things moving as soon as possible.

The following day, I phoned the solicitors to make an appointment to start divorce proceedings. It was time to get the ball rolling and get John out of my life for good.

CHAPTER 16

Coffee with John

I had started divorce proceedings, and everything seemed to be going to plan. A couple of weeks passed, and I received a letter from my solicitor asking me for some documents and suggesting that I drop them in at the office at my earliest convenience. I searched but was unable to find the relevant documents and then realised that they must still be at John's. Reluctantly, I would need to phone John to ask him to look for the paperwork. Since Chris didn't want him coming to the house, I decided that I would arrange to collect it from him. I phoned him and requested that he looked for the relevant documents and get back to me when he had found them to arrange a time to meet. I didn't want to meet him, but it was the only way I was going to get hold of the paperwork.

When we arranged a day and time to meet, he was adamant that he didn't want Chris to be there. Later that day, I informed Chris that I had arranged to meet John. She wondered what time we would be meeting him, and I revealed that John wanted me to go on my own. 'No chance,' she retorted. She didn't want me going on my own and insisted that she was coming with me. I knew he wouldn't meet me if she was there, and I needed the documents.

'Do you know something?' I began. 'I'm sick and tired of this.'

'Sick and tired of what?' Chris wanted to know.

'John won't meet me if you go, and you don't want me to meet him without you being there. I'm stuck in the middle.'

'I'm concerned about your safety.'

I assured her that we would be meeting in a public place, in broad daylight, so everything would be fine. She agreed to step back while I went to meet him.

We had arranged to meet in a café in the centre of town because there were a few things we needed to discuss regarding the house. Chris dropped me off as close to the café as she could then went to Mum's. As I got out of the car, I promised to phone her once I had finished my meeting with John. I walked into the café and over to where John was sitting. He looked at me, smiled, and went to get me a coffee.

'Hello stranger,' he said.

'Hi.'

'You look great! How are you keeping?' he asked.

'I'm fine.'

'I can't believe how different you look! I love the top you're wearing! Is it new?'

'It is actually.'

'Have you put it on specially for meeting me?' he wanted to know, with a smile on his face.

'No, John, I haven't! I don't dress to impress you.'

'No, I forgot, you've got a girlfriend to impress,' he replied, sarcastically.

'If you're going to start being clever, I'm going,' I pointed out to him.

'Do you like my new jumper and trousers?' he wondered, fishing for compliments.

'They're okay,' was all I was prepared to say.

He was wearing a smart pair of grey trousers and a black jumper. He looked nice, but I wasn't going to tell him that.

'I'd like this to be a date,' he said.

'The hell it is! I'm here for one reason only,' I replied in a firm voice.

'How's the relationship going?'

'It couldn't be better.'

'Is she treating you right?' he was keen to know.

'Oh my God, that's rich coming from you.'

'There's no need for sarcasm,' he stated, somewhat defensively.

'Well, I can't believe what you've just said.'

'I just want you to be happy,' he alleged, lowering his voice.

'It's a pity you didn't want that when we lived together.'

'You really do love her, don't you?'

'She's my world! You set out to split us up, but we

knew that it wasn't possible.'

'In that case, I wish you every happiness.'

'I need to get this paperwork taken in. Pass me the envelope please,' I asked.

He pushed the envelope over the table to me. I picked it up and took the paperwork out. I stared at it.

'For God's sake, John, this is not what I requested,' I articulated.

'Oh, sorry,' he replied, with a smug look on his face.

'You've done this deliberately.'

'I just wanted to see you.'

'Chris is going to hit the roof when I tell her,' I informed him.

'Don't tell her,' he suggested.

'Oh, I will be telling her! Unlike you and I, we are honest with each other.'

'Meet me tonight for a drink and I'll bring the correct paperwork.'

'I'm going,' was my reply, as I felt so annoyed with him.

'Don't go,' he urged.

I got up from the table and walked out.

I phoned Chris because I was ready to be picked up. I got into the car, and she wondered if everything was okay. Things were far from okay. She wanted to know why, and I revealed what John had done. She was annoyed. 'So, what happens now?' Chris wanted to know. I didn't know; I still needed the paperwork. We went to Mum's, and I revealed what had happened. She wondered what game he was playing. He was doing what he liked to do best, which was being in control. I had wasted time in town being with an idiot who I didn't want to be with in the first place. I resigned myself to meeting him again as I needed the documents, which was exactly what he wanted. Mum then offered to meet him and get the documents for me. It wasn't a good idea because I didn't trust him. I doubt that he would have agreed to meet Mum anyway. We had lunch and spent the afternoon at Mum's, chatting and putting the world to rights, as you do.

That evening, Chris and I talked. I let her know what John had said - he would have to accept our relationship and wished us every happiness. She looked at me with raised eyebrows, 'Do you think he might have come to his senses and realised he's not going to get you back, and is genuinely happy for us?'

'No, I know him too well. He's up to something. I don't trust him,' I replied.

A couple of days passed, and I phoned John to tell him that I would be coming to collect the documents that evening. He wasn't sure if it was convenient. 'I'm not asking you if it's okay to come down, I'm telling you that I'm calling, so make sure that you're in.' He changed his mind, saying it would be fine, and we made arrangements for 5 pm. He insisted that he didn't want Chris going into the house. Chris and I were going out for dinner that evening, so we would go on for our meal straight from John's. When we arrived at 5 pm, Chris stayed in the car, and I knocked on the door. It seemed to take John ages to answer. He apologised when he finally opened the door and claimed that he had been on the phone talking to his mum. I walked in and he locked the door. I insisted that he left the door unlocked, otherwise I was leaving.

'You look lovely tonight,' he commented.

'We're going out for dinner,' I replied.

'What's the occasion?'

'I just want to take my girlfriend out for dinner. It's what you do when you're in a relationship.'

'Where are you eating?' he wanted to know.

'Nowhere you know,' was my reply.

'I can remember us going out for meals.'

'That seems such a long time ago, John. A lot has happened since then.'

'Where did you say you were going?' he asked again.

'I didn't! Our location for the evening is given to people on a need-to-know basis. You're not one of those people that need to know,' I firmly replied.

'Fine, I was only making conversation.'

'Have you got the paperwork?'

'I'm sorting it now.'

'I haven't got all evening,' I reminded him.

'You look sexy. I often think about you and her in bed.'

'Get a life, John, instead of getting off on it thinking about me and Chris in bed,' I replied, looking at him in disgust.

'I'm envious.'

'Sex is all you think about, John! Get a partner and stop fantasising about your ex-wife's sex life,' I was annoyed that he was having such thoughts.

'Why have you brought Chris?'

'Because she's my partner and we are going out from here.'

'I didn't want her to come,' he retorted, his voice rising.

'No, John, you didn't want her coming into the house, which is why she is sitting outside. There is a difference.'

'She seduced you and broke our marriage up,' he stated, angrily.

'No, John, you broke the marriage up! It was dead long before Chris and I got together,' I reminded him.

'We could start afresh,' he suggested.

'It's not going to happen! I'm not in love with you John, and to be honest, I don't feel that I ever was. I'm gay, and I don't want a relationship with you or any other man.'

'I was a fool to let you go.'

'I want the paperwork now, or I'm walking out,' I demanded.

'It's here,' he said, handing me a large brown envelope.

'You did have it ready then?' I replied, as I checked

the contents.

'I'm still in love with you,' he declared.

'You've got to let it go, John,' I insisted

'I can't move on.'

'I'm going,' I expressed, as I made my way to the door.

'Can I ask you a question before you leave?' he said, as he followed me.

'If you must.'

'Why did you marry me when you were obviously gay?'

'I don't know, John! I loved you as a person, but then realised that I wasn't 'in love' with you. Therefore, we should never have got married.'

'Please don't go,' he begged.

'Everything is sorted now; the divorce is going through, so I won't be contacting you again. I would appreciate it if you didn't make any further contact with me. Any future correspondence will be done through solicitors. Up to now, I think I've been patient with you, but if you contact me again, either directly, or indirectly, I will get an injunction against you,' I firmly stated.

'I've got the message loud and clear.'

'Oh, one last thing before I go.'

'What's that?'

'Quite a while ago you were confident that the relationship between Chris and I wouldn't last, and that you would destroy us. If anything, you have pushed us closer together. For the record we are stronger than ever - and you're still single! Funny how things turn out, John.' I turned on my heel, marched down the hallway, and slammed the door shut behind me.

I got back in the car, and we headed off to the pub. On the way, Chris asked me if everything was okay. I said that it was, but he was hard work. I confirmed that it had been my final meeting with John, and I wouldn't need to contact him again. I had instructed him not to get in touch with me again, so hopefully that would be it, once and for all.

'You do realise that John is still in love with you, and he's not going to let it go,' Chris remarked.

'I know. He has made that clear tonight. He will let it go because I've warned him that if he doesn't, I will take out an injunction against him.'

'Would you do that?'

'Definitely,' I exclaimed.

We headed off to the pub and had a lovely meal. Hopefully, that would be the last we saw of John.

When we returned home, Chris poured us both a drink and we talked. She knew everything there was to know about how things had been within my marriage. She could never understand why I had put up with him for so long. Looking back, I realised that leaving him was the best thing I ever did because the marriage had been dead for a while. He seemed so certain that I would never leave him, and the more certain he was that I wouldn't go, the more determined I was about going.

At the time, I couldn't understand what was happening or why he was being the way he was with me. He had everything, a good job, a lovely home, and a new wife, but it didn't appear to be enough for him. He started spending money like there was no tomorrow and saying that he hadn't been paid at work, when in fact he had. Chris wondered what he had been doing with the money. I knew he was drinking, and I was pretty sure that he was gambling. I couldn't live that way and I wasn't prepared to continue in a relationship full of uncertainty. She always thought there was something about him, but she could never put her finger on it. He needed to get help because the way he was acting certainly wasn't how you would expect someone to act normally.

She then said, 'I want to ask you something.'

'Go ahead,' I replied.

'Did John ever force you to have sex with him?'

I was slightly surprised at her question but assured her that he hadn't. John was many things. He was a liar, a drinker, and he liked to be in control, but he never forced me to have sex with him. I don't believe that he ever would have. He wasn't that type of person. I wouldn't have tolerated that type of behaviour and would have reported him immediately if he had ever tried to force himself on me. I will admit that he would sulk and be offhand with me if I didn't want to have sex with him, but the more he sulked, the more I was determined that I wasn't sleeping with him. 'I'm fed up with talking about him. Let's talk about something else,' I said.

I got up and poured us another drink and Chris

put some music on. We always enjoyed listening to the songs that were playing the first night we spent together, they were our songs. Chris always said that she loved spending time with me, and that I always made her feel so loved and so relaxed. Sometimes we would talk for hours and other times we would just enjoy sitting quietly. If we were together, it didn't matter what we were doing, we were enjoying each other's company. We could have been standing in the middle of a field in the pouring rain and we would have been happy, as long as we were together.

We were having a lovely evening, until the phone rang. Chris answered it, and it was John. He insisted that he wanted to speak to me. Chris was fuming. She asked me if I wanted to speak to him, and I confirmed that I didn't. He insisted that I either speak to him on the phone or he would be coming down. I jumped up from the sofa and went to the phone. 'What the hell are you playing at, John?' I asked, reminding him what I had said when I had seen him earlier that evening. He was harassing me, and I intended taking legal action against him. He advised me that there was no need for that as there was a reason why he had phoned. He had accepted that there was no way back for me and him. Once everything was sorted with the house, he was moving away.

He just wanted to say a final goodbye, and he wished Chris and I lots of luck for the future. I wished him well and suggested that if he ever got involved with anyone else, he needed to treat them a lot better than he had treated me, otherwise it would never work. He agreed and said, 'Look after yourself.'

I replied, 'Goodbye, John, take care.'

I went back into the lounge, and Chris was eager to know what the conversation was about. I revealed what had been said, and she questioned whether I believed him. I did believe him, because for some reason he seemed different from how he had been when I had seen him earlier in the evening. He seemed to be calmer and more collected, and I did feel that he would be finally moving on and making a new life for himself.

He had set out to destroy us, but it hadn't worked. We were rock solid and nothing and no one could come between us. He was powerless. He had lost control of the game he was playing, which was something that he wouldn't have been able to cope with. This was why he needed to move away.

Following that telephone call, we never heard from John again. My divorce was finalised in 1988.

CHAPTER 17

Out on the Town

A few days later, I went into town and bumped into an old friend. We went for a coffee and had a lovely long chat. Lisa remarked on how good I looked, and we talked about what was happening in our lives. When I mentioned that John and I had separated, she didn't seem surprised. 'I think you're well rid of him, to be honest,' she commented. I decided that now was the right time to confide in her, so I took a deep breath and told her that I was in a new relationship and had been for several months. She was eager to know his name.

I replied, 'Her.'

With a surprised look on her face she said, 'Okay, what's her name then?'

I told her, and she asked if I was happy. 'I'm so happy and in love,' I replied, smiling.

'I'm so pleased for you! The relationship is obviously having a good effect on you as you look so much different,' she said.

I was eager to know if it bothered her that I was gay, and she revealed that she already had her suspicions. I wondered why she had never mentioned it before, and she confessed that she had been waiting for me to tell her. She could never understand why I had got married in the first place and had a feeling the marriage wouldn't last. She had never liked John and was surprised I had stayed with him as long as I had.

She suggested a night out in town and wondered if I would be free at the weekend. I promised to give her a call and let her know. I wasn't sure whether Chris had any plans for us at the weekend. We finished our coffee, and I carried on with what I had to do in town, and she went on her way.

When I got home, I mentioned to Chris that I had bumped into an old friend who had invited me out for a drink on Saturday night. She was eager to know if I was going, and I said that I wouldn't mind unless she had plans for us. She didn't have anything planned, so it was fine, and we left it at that, for the time being! Later that evening, we were watching TV and I could see that Chris had the type of look on her face that someone has when they want to ask you something but are unsure whether to.

'How old is she?' Chris questioned.

'My age.'

'Is she married?'

'No!' I quickly replied.

'Is she in a relationship?'

'No,' I said.

At this point Chris went quiet.

'Go on then, ask your next question,' I urged,

smiling at her.

'No, it's fine.'

'Well, I'll answer it for you anyway. As far as I know she's not gay.'

'Well, I was wondering,' she admitted.

'I know you were. It was written all over your face.'

'But you're not 100% sure?'

'I'm 99% sure,' I assured her.

'And it's that 1% that concerns me,' was her reply.

'Look, I'm sure I would know if she was gay.'

'Is it likely to become a regular thing?'

'I wouldn't think so! Would you prefer it if I didn't go?'

'I don't mind at all. I'm happy for you to go.'

A few minutes passed, and she started to ask more questions. She wanted to know where we would be going.

'Just into town,' I replied.

We left it at that. I had mentioned Lisa to Chris in the past, but I hadn't discussed her in detail, and they had never met. I phoned Lisa to let her know that I was free at the weekend, and we arranged a time to meet.

The weekend arrived, and I was getting ready to go out with Lisa. It had been a while since I had been out with a friend, so I was looking forward to the evening. We had arranged to meet at 7:30 pm, and Chris offered to drop me off in town. We set off, and I arrived about fifteen minutes early, so I suggested that Chris dropped me off and went back home. There were plenty of people about, so I wasn't concerned about being in town on my own. However, she wanted to wait until Lisa arrived, so we just sat chatting. I let Chris know that I would probably get home for around 11:30 pm. Right on time, Lisa appeared. I told Chris that she was there.

'Where?'

I pointed her out to Chris, then got out of the car. She rolled the car window down and I said, 'Are you happy now?'

'What do you mean?' she asked.

'Now that you've seen her. You must think I'm stupid.'

She smiled at me, winked, and said, 'Take care, and have a good time.' I walked over to Lisa, and I could sense that Chris was watching me. We gave each other a hug; Chris sounded the horn and slowly drove off.

During the evening, Lisa was curious to know how things were going with me and Chris. I told her that things couldn't be better - Chris was everything I had ever wanted in a partner. She remarked on how happy and relaxed I was, and that ending it with John was the best thing I could have done. Marrying him had been a foolish mistake. It had also been an expensive mistake, all things considered.

We went to a couple of pubs that were playing good music, so we were up dancing and having such a good time. The drinks were flowing, and the more we drank, the more we wanted to dance, and the evening flew. Lisa fancied going to a nightclub, but I wasn't bothered on this occasion, so we just stuck to the pubs. We had a lovely evening; it was great to have a good catch-up. We hadn't seen each other for a while before our coffee in town. I looked at my watch and it was 11 pm so we decided to make our way home. We were both getting a taxi, as I didn't want Chris coming back out once she had got settled at home, although she wouldn't have minded. We had both had quite a few drinks, but we weren't drunk, just merry. I assured Lisa that I would give her a call in a few days, and she said, 'Let's not leave it so long next time.'

She gave me a hug and said, 'Love you.'

'Love you too.' It was what we always said to each other in the friendly sense.

I arrived home and let myself in. As I opened the door to the lounge, Chris just looked at me and gave me a beautiful smile.

'I've missed you,' Chris admitted.

'I didn't think you would still be up.'

'I wasn't going to bed until I knew you were back home safe. Plus, I'm not tired.'

At that point I just looked at Chris with a big grin on my face. She cracked out laughing. 'I can't talk to you when you've had a drink, you always end up making me laugh,' she said.

'What did you think of Lisa?'

'The bit I saw of her, I thought she looked nice,' she replied.

'The bit you saw of her. You had a good look at her! In fact, that's why you didn't want to drop me off and go before she arrived. I'm not stupid.'

'I just wanted to see what she looked like, that's all,' she uttered, smiling at me.

'And?' I said, waiting for her opinion.

'Yes, she looked nice. In fact, I felt quite jealous.'

'Why?'

'Because she was going to be spending the evening with my girlfriend.'

'Yes, but we have all the other evenings together.'

Chris poured us both a glass of wine and we talked while music was playing softly in the background.

'Have you both had a good night?'

'Yes, it's been great! We've had a good catch-up,' I voiced, excitedly.

'Are you going out with her again?'

'I wouldn't mind at some point. Is that going to be a problem?'

'We'll find out, won't we?' she replied.

'What do you mean?'

'Time will tell whether it's going to be a problem.'

'Why are you being like this? She's not a threat to our relationship,' I assured her.

'Are you sure? Something is telling me that she is gay.'

'I'm positive she's not. I've known her since we were at school. I don't think she's gay, and even if she was, it wouldn't make any difference because I'm in a relationship with you, and I love you so much.'

'I know you do.'

'Why are you feeling so insecure?' I asked.

'Probably because of the age difference. You're still young enough to want to go out and have a good time with friends.'

'And how often is that?'

'Very rare,' she replied.

'Exactly! This is the first time I've been out with a friend since we got together,' I reminded her.

'Just ignore me, I've had a few drinks too, so I think that could be kicking in.'

'Our relationship does and will always come first,' I assured her.

'I know, and I love you for that. I trust you 100%. It's other people that I don't trust.'

I poured us both another drink, and as one of our favourite songs was playing, I took hold of Chris's hand, and we slow danced. I started to kiss her. The kiss became more intense, and Chris whispered, 'I think we need to take this upstairs.' I went upstairs, got undressed, and apparently, when Chris came up a few minutes later, I was sprawled out on the bed fast asleep, as she informed me the following morning. Rather than disturb me, she left me on the bed, covered me up, and went and slept in the spare bed.

The following morning Chris brought me a drink and asked how I was feeling. I felt slightly under the weather. I probably shouldn't have had the wine when I got home, as I had felt okay until then, but as soon as I had got on the bed, I was gone. She just winked at me and whispered, 'You can make it up to me later.' She persuaded me to go back to sleep and she would get me up in a couple of hours.

About an hour later, Mum phoned to invite us for lunch. Chris revealed that I was slightly under the weather, and Mum wondered what was wrong. Chris informed her that I had been out with Lisa and then had a couple more drinks when I got home, so I had probably over done it. 'I'll get her to give you a call later, but I think it's doubtful that she will want any lunch,' Chris presumed. I got up late morning and by the time I had showered and dressed, I was feeling fine.

I phoned Mum, and she offered to cook dinner in the evening if we wanted to go. I mentioned it to Chris, and she agreed that it would be lovely to see Mum. We arranged to be there for 5 pm. As we entered Mum's hallway, we were met with the lovely smell of roast beef and homemade Yorkshire puddings. Mum had cooked a beautiful Sunday roast. She wanted to know if I had enjoyed my evening with Lisa, and how she was keeping. I told Mum all about it, saying it had been lovely to see her; we had a great night, but I had ended up having more to drink than I intended. She pointed out that it had been a while since I had seen Lisa, so it must have been good for us to go out and have a catch-up. Then Chris mentioned that I had kept making her laugh when I came home. 'She usually does that when she's had a drink,' Mum replied, with a smile.

While Mum and Chris were having a coffee, they

were talking about some of the funny things I had done in the past. I piped up and said, 'I'm still here, you know.' They just looked at me and smiled. I went into the kitchen to make a drink, and they continued talking. I could hear Mum telling Chris that Lisa and I were best friends at school, and that we had remained friends since. Mum was telling Chris how she used to love putting my hair in pigtails for school, at which point I thought, *Just shoot me now! Mum is in reminiscing mode - any time now the school photographs are going to come out.* Thankfully, they didn't. Chris still had that to come! We spent about another hour with Mum and then went home. We had enjoyed being with Mum, and as always, she had cooked a beautiful meal. As far as I was concerned, Mum's Sunday roast was the best.

I lay on the sofa, and Chris lifted my legs up, sat down and put my legs across hers. She had poured us a glass of wine and started talking about when we first got together. I reminded her that she had taken a chance with the hug that she gave me, and she certainly took a chance kissing me. She didn't know for certain that I was gay and could quite easily have ended up with a slap that night. She admitted that it was a chance that she was prepared to take as she was besotted with me. She would have gladly taken a slap, because at least she would have had the satisfaction of kissing me. She had got some bottle, as I would never attempt to kiss another woman on the lips if I wasn't in a relationship with her. She grabbed the opportunity because she had a pretty good idea that I would respond in a favourable way. She could sense that there was an attraction from both sides. I pointed out to her that she could have got things so wrong, but she was pretty sure that she hadn't.

She loved everything about me, especially my eyes. She loved the colour of them and always said that they were sexy. She was surprised that I hadn't noticed how she used to look at my eyes when we were talking in the pub. She couldn't help herself. Thinking back, she did seem to look deep into my eyes when we were talking. When you look back, it's funny how you can recognise things that you didn't necessarily pick up on at the time.

She had her suspicions that I was gay. When you are gay yourself, it's relatively easy to suss out women who are gay, although it's not always apparent. She reminded me how she knew right from the start what she wanted and that it was me who took some time making my mind up and coming to terms with the situation. Which of course was true. My head was a mess at that time, because there were a lot of things going on with me and John. She wondered why it took me so long to decide if I wanted a relationship with another woman, as I was obviously gay. I needed to be certain that she was the right one for me. She reminded me that she was so much in love and would never have given up on me, no matter how long it took. She wondered if I had any regrets about being in the relationship. 'I have only one regret,' I said softly.

Her face changed, she looked at me and said, 'What's that?'

Smiling, I replied, 'That I didn't meet you sooner.'

She leaned over and kissed me. We finished our wine and went to bed; I had some making up to do for falling asleep the previous evening.

Everything was great within our relationship. We hadn't heard anything from John for weeks, which pleased us both. I think the mention of getting an injunction against him if he contacted me again may have done the trick. Or possibly he could be in a new relationship himself, though he needed to drastically change his ways if he was ever going to get anyone to stay with him long term.

Chris and I were in a good place, I was now with a partner who I was so much in love with, and I couldn't possibly imagine life without her. She was the one who I had always been looking for. She loved me so much. She made me happy, and she made me feel alive. However, something happened, and she also made me question whether I still wanted to be in a relationship with her!

CHAPTER 18

Troubled Waters

On a Thursday evening, Chris picked me up from work. While we were chatting, she remembered Lisa had phoned and wanted me to call her back. We arrived home. I had a drink and a shower, then I phoned Lisa. She wondered if I was free at the weekend, as she had been given some tickets to see a band at one of the nightclubs in town. I wasn't too sure whether I would be able to make it but promised to let her know. I mentioned it to Chris, and she asked if I was going. That depended on her, and whether she felt comfortable with it. She shrugged her shoulders and said it was fine with her if I wanted to go.

The following morning, I phoned Lisa and we arranged a time to meet. She suggested that Chris came with us because it would give them the opportunity to meet and get to know each other. I thought it was a great idea because I would have loved her to come with us, but I knew that she wouldn't go as she wasn't keen on drinking in town. I mentioned it to Chris, but she wasn't bothered about going, which is exactly what I thought she would say. I didn't put pressure on her; she didn't want to go so I just left it at that.

The evening arrived, and I was getting ready to go out. I had showered and was choosing the clothes that I would be wearing. I had been in the bedroom a few minutes when the door opened, and Chris came in. She lay on the bed, and we were chatting while I was getting dressed. She said, 'Come and lie at the side of me.'

'I would love to, but we both know what it will lead to, and time is getting on,' I replied. I suggested that she went back downstairs as she was a distraction. The temptation was there, but we needed to be leaving shortly. She left the room, and I finished getting dressed.

She was going to visit her sister for a couple of hours, so she would drop me off in town and go on from there. I told her that there was no need for her to hang around in town this time, as she had already seen what Lisa looked like when we had previously gone out. 'Do I detect a hint of sarcasm in that statement?' Chris replied.

'Sorry, I couldn't resist,' I said, smiling.

I suggested that she didn't wait up for me as I would probably get home quite late. She wondered what time it was likely to be, and I confirmed that it would be well after midnight. I wondered if she was okay with that. 'It's fine! Have a good time!' she said as she dropped me off.

We had a great evening. The band was good, and they also played disco music, so we were up dancing. We talked, we danced, and we reminisced about our school days. I suggested that Lisa came to see Mum some time as they always got on well when we were at school. I knew Mum would love to see her. She reminded me how she used to love coming to my house when my father was out. Mum always made her welcome and made a fuss of her. There were numerous 'Can you remember when ...' moments as we looked back on our school days. It had been a lovely evening, with good company and a great atmosphere. However, the evening seemed to be over before we knew it, and it was time to get a taxi home. I arrived home at 1:15 am, and as expected, Chris was waiting up for me. I opened the door to the lounge, and Chris just looked at me over the top of her glasses. I thought, *Oops -she doesn't look happy!*

'Hi!' I said, smiling at her.

'What time do you call this?'

'I call it 1:15 am, why, what time do you call it?' I replied, jokingly.

'Don't be clever, I'm not in the mood.'

'And there's me hoping that you would be in the mood.'

'You've got no chance,' her voice was sharp, and she looked annoyed.

'What's the problem? I told you I would be late home.'

'I didn't expect it to be this late.'

'Am I on a curfew or something?' I asked, with raised eyebrows.

'Of course not.'

'What's wrong?'

'I think Lisa is gay,' she replied.

'For God's sake, not this again,' I retorted.

'Tell me the truth! Is she gay?' she insisted.

'I'm telling you the truth. As far as I know, she isn't gay.'

'I have a strong feeling that she is.'

Chris wouldn't let the subject go.

At this point she was starting to make me question my own thoughts about Lisa. One of us was right about her sexuality and one of us was wrong, but I didn't know which one it was. I was pretty sure that Lisa wasn't gay, but could I be wrong? On the other hand, Chris seemed pretty sure that she was gay, but could she be wrong?

'Should I go out and come back in?'

'Why don't you go one better? Go and stay at hers! You've been with her all evening, so why not finish the night off properly?'

'I don't need this! You knew I would be late home and at the time you didn't have a problem with it. I even asked you to come with us, but you declined,' I retorted.

'Because I didn't want to go.'

'This has got nothing to do with what time I came home. I've been out all evening with a single female, who you think is gay. That's what this is all about.' I was now feeling frustrated.

'Does she want a relationship with you?'

'Not that I'm aware of. Even if she did, it wouldn't be happening because I'm with you. You've got this so wrong, Chris! This all boils down to insecurity.'

'Are you wishing we had never got together?'

'No, Chris, I'm not, but I am wishing I had never gone out.'

'I can't handle you going out with other women, even though they are only friends.'

'If you hadn't wanted me to go, you should have said.'

'And would you have stayed at home if I had?' she was eager to know.

'Probably! But you need to understand that I am entitled to a life outside our relationship, just as you are.'

'So where does this leave things?' she asked, while pouring a drink.

'To be honest, Chris, right at this moment, I don't know. I'm certainly not putting up with this,' I firmly replied.

'I love you so much and I'm scared of losing you.'

'Carry on the way you are and there won't be a relationship between us.'

'And would you be happy to walk away from what we have?'

'Of course not, but I don't want things to be like this.'

'Are you ending the relationship?' she wondered.

'No, Chris, I'm not! But you need to have a good think about your actions this evening and decide exactly what you want.'

'I don't want us to break up,' she assured me.

'I don't want to break up either, but the way you have been tonight has made me question whether there is a future for us,' I said, raising my voice.

'I'm so sorry,' she uttered, as she walked towards me.

'We'll talk in the morning. I'm tired and I'm going to bed.'

'Are you annoyed with me?'

'Annoyed? Chris, I'm absolutely fuming! I don't expect to come home to this after an innocent night out with a friend,' I shouted, while making my way upstairs.

'Do you want me to sleep in the spare bed?' she wondered.

'That's entirely up to you,' I replied.

I couldn't believe how rapidly the situation had escalated. This was unusual behaviour for Chris. I went to bed wondering what the following day would bring as there seemed to be a lot of uncertainty based around our relationship. I certainly didn't want the relationship to end, but things needed to change. Chris slept in the spare bed. She knew that she had overstepped the mark. I woke up around 9 am the following morning and discovered Chris was lying at the side of me. I found it amusing how we had gone to sleep in separate beds yet woken up in the same bed. Chris later told me she had got in with me a couple of hours after we had gone to bed. It felt good, and it was lovely to wake up and feel her close to me. I was the first to get up, showered and dressed, followed by Chris an hour later. I needed to clear my head, so I decided to go for a long walk, on my own.

I returned home and walked into the lounge. Chris looked at me and said, 'I'm sorry!' I informed her that I had decided to go to Mum's for a few hours as I felt that we needed some space. She made us both a drink and we talked about the previous evening. She had been out of order, and I didn't particularly want to be around her. She apologised and I advised that the best apology she could give me would be to get her act together and stop feeling insecure.

I phoned Mum and asked if it was okay to call, which of course it was. She wondered if everything was alright, and I told her that I just needed some space for a few hours. Chris begged me not to go, but I felt that it was for the best. She put her arms around me, said that she loved me and asked me if I still loved her. I assured her that I loved her, and nothing would ever stop me loving her, but things did need to change. We both needed some breathing space and being at Mum's would be as much for her benefit as it was for mine. She would be able to focus on what she needed to address easier if I wasn't there. She offered to drop me at Mum's, and I told her that I was more than happy to get the bus.

'I want to drop you off,' she stated.

'I bet you do, because that way you'll know that I've not gone to see Lisa,' I replied.

She said nothing. I mentioned that I would be contacting Lisa at some point because I wanted some answers. This needed sorting out as it was having an impact on our relationship, which was something that neither of us were happy about.

On the way to Mum's, I reminded Chris that what we had was special, but she was spoiling it. I got out of the car, went into Mum's, and burst into tears. Mum put her arms around me and gave me a hug. Just getting a hug from Mum always seemed to make things that much better. She was eager to know what was wrong. I revealed that Chris and I were having one or two problems, but I didn't go into all the finer details. I did tell her that Chris was convinced that Lisa was gay and wanted more than just friendship. At that point Mum wanted to know if I thought that Lisa was gay. I said that I hadn't thought so initially, but Chris was making me question my own thoughts. I spent a couple of hours with Mum and then decided to get the bus home, rather than asking Chris to pick me up.

On the way home, I stopped at the phone box. I needed to speak to Lisa, but I didn't want to make the call from Mum's. There were questions I wanted answers to. I needed to get this sorted quickly as Chris would be at home on her own, wondering whether she had blown things between us, which didn't sit well with me. I was regretting going to Mum's and felt that I should have stayed at home with Chris. I was missing her and wanted to get back home to her.

Lisa answered the phone and I decided to broach the subject straight away.

'I'm going to ask you a question, and I would like an honest answer.'

'Go ahead,' Lisa replied.

'Are you gay?' I asked, nervously.

'Is it you who wants to know or is it Chris?'

'Both of us,' I stated.

'Do you think I'm gay?'

'Well, I didn't, but I'm now starting to wonder,' I replied, curiously.

'Would it make a difference to our friendship if I was?'

'Not as far as I'm concerned. Chris would have a problem dealing with it.'

'If I was gay, where would that leave us?'

'It would leave us exactly where we are now, nothing more. Stop playing games with me, Lisa, and tell me,' I urged.

'No, I'm definitely not gay! Even if I was, I would never try to come between you and Chris because I know how happy you are and how much you love each other.'

'No one could ever come between us,' I assured her.

'I would give anything to have what you and Chris have got.'

'She's my world, Lisa, and I'm so in love with her.'

'She's good for you. I've not seen you this happy for a long time! You two were made for each other,' she stated, affectionately.

I thanked Lisa for being honest with me, the conversation ended, and I made my way home. I was missing Chris and wanted to put my arms around her and hold her close to me. I arrived home and informed

Chris that I had spoken to Lisa. She was eager to know if I had managed to get the answers I wanted. I revealed that Lisa had said that she wasn't gay, confirming what I knew all along, and that Lisa had stated that even if she were gay, she would never have tried to come between us. 'You need to appreciate that we have been friends for around fifteen years, I know her, and I know she would never have done anything to ruin my relationship with you,' I said, looking into Chris's eyes.

At that point, Chris apologised for getting things so wrong. She felt more at ease now that she knew for certain that Lisa wasn't gay. I wanted to know if Chris had managed to do some thinking while we had been apart, and she assured me that she had. Being with me was all that she had wanted, for a long time, and she was scared of this new life being taken away from her, which was why she was feeling insecure.

'Do you realise how difficult it was for me, being in love with someone who didn't initially have any feelings for me?' Chris said.

'It must have been difficult.'

'I was in love with you long before we got together.'

'So I gather,' I replied, smiling at her.

'You were all I could think about, you had taken over my world.'

'Don't ever feel insecure. This relationship is for keeps,' I assured her.

'I know, and I have addressed the issue,' she assured me.

'You know how much I risked in order to be with you?'

'I know, you risked a lot.'

'I didn't know how Mum would take the news. I also risked losing friends, so I didn't go into it lightly,' I reminded her.

'All I wanted was for us to be together.'

'Maybe we should have taken things even slower than we did,' I suggested.

'I couldn't,' she declared, looking at me with eyes full of love.

'No - you couldn't keep your bloody hands off me,' I whispered, as I kissed her.

She knew how much I loved her, and that there was no reason for her to have feelings of insecurity. She asked if we were okay, and I assured her that as far as I was concerned, we were fine. There were bound to be times when we disagreed and had arguments, but it didn't mean we loved each other any less.

Chris went into the kitchen to pour us both a glass of wine and came back into the lounge with a beautifully wrapped box of chocolates and a card that read, 'I Love You.' I was overwhelmed and got emotional. I asked her what they were for, and she stated that she had been out of order, and they were just to say, 'Sorry'. I gave her a kiss and thanked her. I winked at her and suggested making her a list of the different chocolates that I liked so she could refer to it after any future arguments. She smiled and said, 'Don't push it.' It had been a long emotional day, but I was at home with the one I loved, and I felt in a good place. I just wanted to spend the evening talking to Chris and relaxing.

Chris wanted to know what Lisa was like when we were growing up, about family life and things like that. She was the best friend I ever had at school, and we did lots together when I was allowed. She knew what Mum and I went through with my father and how he used to make me stay in if I had been a minute late home the previous night, or if I had looked at him the wrong way; it didn't take much. She was always there for me, and we had been more like sisters than friends. Lisa's house had been our first port of call one night after my father had hit Mum. Lisa had been alongside me at a time in my life when things were difficult for me at home. I needed to know whether Chris would still have a problem with me continuing to have the odd night out with Lisa, and she assured me that it wouldn't be a problem at all, now that things were sorted.

I didn't want to lose contact with Lisa, but if at any point things changed and she started to cause problems for us, I would sever all ties with her. We had a special friendship, and I was confident that Lisa wouldn't jeopardise that.

Weeks passed and I hadn't had another night out with Lisa, although I had spoken to her on the phone. She was now in a relationship herself - with a man. We eventually lost touch as we were both getting on with our lives.

CHAPTER 19

Gay Scene

O f course, when you are in a gay relationship there are lots of raised eyebrows and disgruntled looks from people. Chris and I would go out to pubs, or for a meal, and on occasions we could feel that we were being watched. It was as though people were trying to work out - are they, or aren't they? I could never understand why people used to stare at us as we never displayed our feelings for each other in public. It was something that we swore we would never do, unless it was in a gay pub. However, that didn't stop the staring and the whispering.

On one occasion, we had gone to a pub for a meal. A couple, sitting a few feet away from us, seemed to be fixated with us, to the point where they were unable to concentrate on their own meals. We finished our meal before they did and decided to leave because they were making us feel quite uncomfortable. However, on the way out, I stopped off at their table and told them that I would put them out of their misery. 'Yes, we are a couple,' I confirmed. 'Now we've cleared that up, you might be able to enjoy your meal.'

Leaving the slightly red-faced couple to finish

their meal, I walked out, without banging into anything or catching any article of clothing on the door handle, which is always a bonus.

In the car park, Chris said, 'I can't believe you just did that.'

'Well, I'm sick of people like them,' I replied.

We both started laughing. Chris had also noticed that they had been constantly staring at us. I personally felt that it was unnecessary behaviour. It was those types of incidents that we didn't want to have to deal with and shouldn't have had to. If anything, situations like that just made us stronger.

We were rock solid, and nothing and no one could come between us. We had Mum's support right from day one. She was brilliant, but we never had that level of support from Chris's family, as there was only ever one member of her family who fully accepted that we were a couple. It didn't appear to matter how long Chris and I had been together, certain members of her family just wouldn't accept our relationship. One of Chris's family members once claimed that if ever they were in a pub and Chris and I walked in, they would get up and walk out. When you hear a statement like that from a member of your family, you start to wonder if you are ever going to be accepted in society. You always assume that you are going to have full support from your own family, but in Chris's case, it wasn't to be.

At that point, we decided to do some research into what the local gay scene had to offer, and we started going to a gay pub and nightclub in Sheffield. At first, spending the evening in a gay pub felt strange, as this was a new experience for both of us. Before I went into a gay pub for the first time, I was nervous. The idea of walking into the pub was bothering us, or should I say it was bothering me more than it was Chris. However, after quite a bit of dithering about outside, we went in and thankfully it was a nice pub, and the people were welcoming.

We continued going every weekend and also started going to a nightclub, which was within walking distance from the pub. It was good that we could be ourselves and not have to worry about people passing judgement. It was a lively nightclub, and it was regularly 3 am before we returned home if we had been there at the weekend. We met some lovely people in Sheffield. We got friendly with a couple of people and stayed at their house on occasions following an evening out. One friend, Sarah, who we used to meet in the pub if she wasn't working, invited us to stay overnight at her house instead of going back home. She was going to be staying out herself so at the end of the evening, she took us to her house, gave us the keys, told us to treat it like our own place, and promised she would take us home the following morning.

We also found a gay pub in our local town which we started going to on a weekly basis. This was better for us as we didn't have to travel to Sheffield every weekend. The first time we went into our local gay pub, we were slightly apprehensive as it wasn't our usual venue. To be honest, I was more nervous about going in the gay pub in our own town than I was when I went into the ones in Sheffield.

We bought our drinks and sat at a table. We

didn't know anyone, so we were just observing the surroundings and chatting between ourselves. We hadn't been there long when this guy came over to our table and introduced himself, which we thought was a nice thing to do. He told us that he usually stood at the bar with some other friends and invited us to join them. He introduced us to a few other people and in time we became good friends with them. This was good, we had found a local gay pub, with a great atmosphere and we felt comfortable. We started going in every Saturday night, and occasionally on a Sunday night when there was disco music playing. It was a place where we could relax and be ourselves, and we enjoyed seeing our new friends and spending time with them.

In your own town, you start to wonder who you might see in the gay pubs, and sure enough, we did see people we recognised, but didn't know were gay. It was probably the same on both sides, as they wouldn't have previously known that we were gay. It's surprising how many straight people you see in gay pubs, or should I say they claim to be straight! It was quite an eye-opener as we would see people in the gay pub at the weekend with same-sex partners, and at a later date, we would see one or two of them in town with their heterosexual partners. Whatever floats your boat, I'm not here to judge.

I was enjoying the music, which was being played in the gay pubs, more so than Chris. She liked music, but she didn't share the same passion for it as I did, and still do. I started to collect certain songs, which I purchased from music stores in Pontefract and Chesterfield. We got friendly with the DJ from the gay pub in our local town who we occasionally took to Pontefract with us so he could purchase new music to play in the pub. We were loving the life we were living, the people we were meeting, and had made such a lot of new friends. We were enjoying all that the gay scene had to offer - the nightlife, the dance music, and the atmosphere in most of the venues that we visited. This was a new way of socialising for us, and we were having a blast.

We also had a couple of weekends away in Blackpool, where we stayed in a guest house owned by a gay couple. It was a lovely place, catering predominantly, but not exclusively, for gay guests. We got on well with the female owners, and they pointed us in the right direction of the best gay bars to visit, and the ones to steer clear of. We met up with them one evening in one of the bars that they had recommended and had a good night. We ended the evening with a drink with them when we got back to the guest house.

It was a great weekend, and it was the first time that Chris and I had been away together, so that made the weekend even more special. We did return to the same guest house at a later date, but this time we invited Mum to come with us. She jumped at the idea, although I did point out to her that the guest house we would be staying in was run by a gay couple and would be more than likely occupied by gay visitors. It didn't bother her in the slightest, and she said that she was more than happy to stay there. We didn't visit any of the gay bars on this occasion as we wanted to take Mum to a regular pub for a meal, though I'm pretty sure she wouldn't have minded visiting a gay bar. It was great taking Mum with us; she got on well with the owners of the guest house and the other guests, and we all had a lovely weekend.

Chris and I once went to Manchester for the day as we wanted to go shopping in a different city. We had a great time, looking around some of the sights, and Chris took me for a lovely lunch. While we were in Manchester, we had a walk along Canal Street. This was something we had always wanted to do. For those of you who aren't familiar with Canal Street, it is also known as Manchester Gay Village. It is a pedestrianised street lined with gay bars and restaurants.

Since it was daytime, there were very few people around, though it was still enjoyable to have a leisurely walk along the street, looking at the many different bars. I could imagine that for the gay community, it would be a good night out. Of course, I wouldn't have thought that heterosexual customers would have been turned away from any of the bars if they had wanted to spend the evening there. Both Chris and I said that we would like to spend a weekend in Manchester at some point so that we were able to experience the nightlife on Canal Street. It was something that we always wanted to do. Unfortunately, we never returned.

I'm unsure how some people perceive gay women, but I think they are of the opinion that all lesbians are butch. I beg to differ. There are some attractive, feminine gay women around, and you would never guess that they were gay. Similarly, there are some handsome, butch men around that you would never suspect were gay. A night in a gay bar or nightclub is a real eye-opener, as you will encounter people from all walks of life.

Yes, you will see butch women, maybe wearing

a shirt and tie, but you will also see feminine women, probably wearing a dress. I personally would not want to be approached by a gay woman who was butch, and certainly not wearing a shirt and tie. I would find it a real turn-off to be honest, and you wouldn't see me for dust. Not that I have anything against them as people, it's just my choice. Oh, and for the record, not all gay women are attracted to every female they see. Just as heterosexuals aren't attracted to every person of the opposite sex that they set eyes on.

This was our new way of life now, and both Chris and I were so happy and enjoying the experience of having a night out in a gay bar. We were able to be affectionate towards each other if we chose to, without being judged. It was a place where we could feel comfortable and be ourselves, which was something we could never have done in a straight bar. Happy days!

CHAPTER 20

Devastating News

C hris was thirty-eight when we first got together. When she was in her mid-forties, she became ill. She had started to experience slight chest tightness but wasn't overly concerned about it at the time. She assured me that she would visit her GP if the condition worsened.

While we were lying in bed one night, my head was resting on Chris's chest, and I noticed that her heart was beating irregularly. Something didn't sound right, and I was concerned. I asked her if she was feeling alright, and she told me that she felt fine. I emphasised that I wasn't happy and that it would be a good idea to make an appointment with her GP. The next morning, she phoned the surgery and was offered an appointment for later that day. The GP examined her. He wasn't too happy with the way her heart sounded and advised her to go to the hospital that day for an x-ray. He gave her a letter to be handed to the receptionist and off she went. Following the x-ray, we came home and didn't think any more of it. However, later that day she received a phone call from the hospital saying that she had a pulmonary embolism. We were stunned. We could not believe this was happening. It can be life-threatening if not treated quickly. She was admitted to hospital straight away, where she remained for a few days as intravenous blood thinning medication needed to be administered.

She was also referred to the Cardiology Out-patients Department where she would have further tests. She was diagnosed with angina and informed that her condition would be monitored. She seemed okay when taking the medication; everything was under control at first, but then she started getting further chest tightness and was referred to the Northern General Hospital in Sheffield. They told her that the angina had worsened. They would be taking over Chris's care, and she was required to attend for regular check-ups. This went on for a few months, but her angina pains were becoming more frequent. After many trips to the Northern General Hospital, she was diagnosed with severe angina. This led to her having numerous hospital tests and procedures up to the point where the consult-ant advised that she needed a coronary artery bypass graft. We looked at each other in shock and disbelief when he gave us this news.

The consultant explained everything that the surgery would entail, which included the benefits and risks of the operation. The benefits being that she would be free from the angina pain and therefore have a better quality of life. The main risk was that she could suffer a heart attack during surgery or shortly afterwards. We were being given worrying information, but we needed to know everything that the operation entailed, includ-ing all the risks. The consultant stated that he knew there was a lot of information for us to process and that Chris would obviously need time to digest that information. He asked Chris if it was likely that she would agree to the surgery. All she could say was that we needed to talk things through. He advised that it would be in her best interest to go ahead with the surgery, and we were given lots of literature to take away. It explained everything in detail.

We had a long chat about the situation over the following few days. It was obvious her condition would not improve without surgery and would only go on to get worse. All things considered, Chris decided to go ahead with the surgery. It had been a difficult decision for her to make, but we both knew that her quality of life would be vastly improved once she had fully recovered from the operation. She also knew that I would be supporting her every step of the way. She contacted the hospital and was placed on the waiting list for triple heart bypass surgery. We couldn't believe this was happening. She was only forty-five and was about to have major heart surgery, but it was surgery that she needed to have. We had to try and prepare for her going into hospital, though it was difficult. How do you prepare for a major operation like that? We didn't know how we were ever going to cope, and it was a worrying time for us. I loved Chris so much and I was hurting inside at the thought of everything that she would have to go through.

The hospital letter finally arrived, and she was given a pre-op assessment date and a date to be admitted. She was required to go into hospital two days prior to having surgery as they needed to monitor her condition and regulate her medication. They also needed to make sure that she was stable in order to undergo surgery. The surgeon had spoken to us at length, telling us what to expect and we had been shown around the Cardiac Intensive Care Unit so that we were familiar with how it looked, and what to expect once Chris was on the ward. We were as prepared as we could be, but the fear of the unknown was ever-present.

She went into hospital and all the usual tests and procedures were done prior to surgery. The surgeon had been up to the ward to have a lengthy chat with Chris and explain everything that would be happening in the operating theatre. Everything was in place, and she was due to go into theatre the following morning. However, an emergency heart transplant patient was admitted, Chris's operation was postponed, and she was sent home. We appreciated that heart transplant surgery would take priority over heart bypass surgery. Although this was frustrating for Chris, we were pleased that a suitable heart had been found for the patient who had been admitted, and we wished them well.

A week later, Chris was given a new date for surgery, which meant that she would have to go through the trauma of getting herself into the right mindset for surgery once again. As before, she was admitted to the hospital a couple of days prior to the operation. The day of surgery arrived, and I wanted to be at the hospital so that I could see Chris before she went down to theatre. Fortunately, I managed to get a lift to the hospital and was there for 7 am. Chris was all prepped and ready for theatre, but I was able to spend some time with her before the porter arrived to collect her. I was allowed to go part of the way with her as she was wheeled down to theatre. Funnily enough, Chris was quite calm and collected, but I was a bag of nerves. I had gone as far as I was permitted to go with her so I kissed her, told her how much I loved her, and assured her that I would be waiting on the ward when she came back up from theatre. They continued on their way, and I broke down. One of the nurses who had come down with us gave me a hug, took me up to the ward, and made me a cup of strong tea. It was going to be a long, stressful day!

The nurse knew that I was going to be staying at the hospital all day, so she took me up to the Cardiac Intensive Care Unit. There was a room, which was a bit further down from the actual ward, but still on the unit, where relatives were able to relax while they waited. *RELAX?* I thought. *No chance!* I'm surprised I didn't wear the carpet out in that room with the number of times I paced up and down. It was a lovely room with comfortable seating and facilities for making refreshments. Mum joined me around mid-morning and brought sandwiches as we didn't want to leave the unit. Time went on and there was no sign of Chris. I couldn't understand why she hadn't come back up from theatre. I knew that before the operation commenced, they would have to stop her heart in order to be able to work on it and she would be placed on a heart-lung machine which would take over the function of the heart and lungs during the procedure. Then I started to think, what if her heart didn't restart, or what if she has suffered a heart attack, which was one of the risk factors. I knew I was starting to get things out of all proportion, but at that time there were a lot of 'what if's' filling my head. Each time I heard the lift open, I went into the corridor to see if it was Chris, but there was no sign of her. Mum said, 'For God's sake, please sit down and I'll make you a drink.' I did as Mum requested but was still constantly watching the door from where I was sitting.

Finally, Chris was brought up from theatre after being down there for around eight hours. I managed to get a quick glimpse of her as she was taken into the ward. She looked awful. Obviously, I didn't expect her to look good when she came back up from theatre as she had undergone major heart surgery, but I didn't expect her to look as ill as she did. It was a while before we were allowed to go in to see her. We seemed to be waiting forever. Finally, a nurse came into the room where Mum and I were. She looked at me, noticed I was tearful, and gave me a hug. I was so pleased to see her - she was our friend, Sarah, who lived in Sheffield and worked on the Cardiac Intensive Care Unit. We used to occasionally meet up with her on a Saturday evening if she wasn't working, and we had stayed at her house a couple of times. She knew that Chris was due to go in for heart surgery and had promised me that Chris would be in good hands.

Sarah took Mum and I in to see Chris, and we were met by numerous machines surrounding Chris, all of which seemed to be making a different noise. She was on a ventilator, and there were tubes attached to her chest to drain off any excess fluid that may build up in the chest cavity. There seemed to be tubes and lines coming out of everywhere. It was distressing to see. Sarah explained to us what all the different tubes and machines were for and told us that Chris was still heavily sedated. I was very emotional; I was relieved that she had come through the surgery okay, but she had such a long way to go. I wanted to put my arms around her and give her the biggest hug ever, but I knew it wasn't possible. She was lying there looking so unwell, and there was nothing that I could do. I felt useless! The job of caring for Chris had been taken out of my hands and put into someone else's, but I knew they would do an excellent job in caring for her. I was there to comfort her, yet she was unaware of my presence.

I appreciated the fact that we had looked around the ward prior to Chris having surgery, but when someone you love is on the ward, and they are attached to all the different monitors, you look at the ward through completely different eyes. I felt fine looking around with Chris and the nurse prior to the operation, but now that Chris was on the ward, I wasn't coping with it too well. Nothing prepares you for when it's your loved one in one of those beds.

The following day, Chris would be allowed to drink clear fluids and receive solid foods if she was able to tolerate them. She also started breathing and coughing exercises, which were an important measure for reducing the risk of lung complications such as pneumonia. Those exercises were extremely painful. Chris later said it felt as though her chest was being crushed. In hospital, the patients who had undergone coronary artery bypass graft surgery were advised by the nursing staff to place a pillow on their chest and press on it slightly to alleviate the pain from coughing. This proved to be a valuable piece of equipment over the coming weeks.

While we were at Chris's bedside, the surgeon came up to check that everything was as it should be. He was a lovely man. I had met him several times before when Chris had seen him in the outpatients' department. He confirmed that everything had gone well with the surgery and that she would remain on the Cardiac Intensive Care Unit as the next forty-eight hours would be critical. She would then be transferred to the ward where she had been to start off with. We were shattered, and Sarah said that we needed to go home and get some rest, and of course she was right. I had been at the hospital for fourteen hours, and it had been a long, traumatic day. Previously, she had invited me to stay with her while Chris was in hospital. Since she lived in Sheffield, it would have made commuting easier. I was grateful for her offer but declined as I wanted to stay at Mum's.

Mum and I agreed that we needed to go home and get some sleep. I kissed Chris before we left and told her that I loved her. She was still out of it, bless her, but I hoped that she had heard me. It was quite late when we arrived home, but we needed to wind down, so we sat up talking for a while. I was emotional and just kept breaking down, which Mum had been expecting once we got home. I phoned the hospital before we went to bed, just to check that everything was still okay with Chris - and of course it was!

When I got up the following morning, the first thing I did was phone the hospital again. The nurse stated that Chris was awake and doing fine. I was so relieved. Later that morning Mum and I set off for the hospital and arrived on the ward to find Chris asleep.

The nurse made us a drink, and we sat at the side of the bed waiting for Chris to wake up. We had been sitting there about twenty-five minutes when she opened her eyes and looked at me. I winked at her and said, 'I love you.' She gave me a lovely smile, and it was so uplifting to see her awake and responsive. I asked her how she was feeling, and she said, 'Rough.' I held her hand. I was so chuffed that she was awake and talking.

The following day, Chris went back to the Cardiac ward, which was where she would remain until she was discharged. It was lovely to see her in a normal ward and no longer attached to so many machines. Each morning, I would phone the ward to enquire about Chris before we visited. One day when Mum and I went to visit, we arrived on the ward to find Chris's bed was empty and had fresh bedding on. My heart sank. Where was she? What had happened? Had she been taken ill while we were on the way to the hospital? Obviously, the hospital wouldn't have been able to contact us once we had left home as we didn't have a mobile phone in those days. Mum noticed that the colour just drained from me when I saw the empty bed. I went to speak to the nurse, and she informed me that Chris had gone out with the physiotherapist to do some exercises. I breathed a huge sigh of relief!

A few minutes later, Chris came back into the ward holding the arm of the physiotherapist. Her face lit up when she saw me and Mum, and we both gave her a big hug, although we had to be very gentle. She had been walking up and down a few stairs where it was quiet, not many, maybe four or five. The physiotherapist explained that it was part of the rehabilitation programme. I thought, *Bloody hell, it's a bit soon for her to be going up and down stairs!* However, they were the professionals and knew what they were doing. I just wanted to wrap Chris in cotton wool, but I knew she needed to be up and about and doing the exercises.

There would be a lot of healing as they had sawn through her sternum in theatre in order to get to her heart properly to perform the surgery. They then realigned the sternum and reconnected it with metal wires which would stay inside her chest permanently. If that wasn't bad enough, she also had quite a lengthy wound on her leg from where they had taken the vein out before they had connected it to her heart. I loved her so much and hated seeing her like this, but I knew that the long-term outlook would be a better quality of life for Chris. We just had to be patient. She was in hospital for ten days and I went to see her every day. I was missing her so much and I wanted her back home with me, where she belonged. The doctors and nurses providing Chris's care had all been brilliant. They had done an excellent job in caring for her.

Finally, the day of discharge arrived. I was so excited! I had been home to put the heating on as I wanted the house to be nice and warm when Chris came home. The temperature in hospital had been constant, so I didn't want her walking into a cold house. I had also bought her a beautiful bouquet, so I wanted to place the flowers in water so they would remain fresh for when Chris got home. When we arrived at the hospital, Chris was dressed and waiting for medication to take home. We had quite a wait as there were a lot of items that needed to come up from the pharmacy. The nurse and a physiotherapist had a long chat with us regarding dos and don'ts at home as part of Chris's rehabilitation. Finally, the medication arrived, and it was time for me to take Chris home. It was the day that I had been longing for. I was so happy!

CHAPTER 21

The Road to Recovery

Chris was back home. As soon as she saw the flowers I had bought for her, tears started to roll down her cheeks. Her emotions were all over the place at that time, and she seemed to be very weepy. I put my arms around her and hugged her gently. I didn't want to hug her too tightly because of the surgery she had just had. She had been informed at the hospital that full recovery would take up to twelve weeks, so this is where the journey began.

I made sure she was comfortable on the sofa and made her a coffee. She was tired as the day had been a bit of an ordeal for her. I suggested that she went to bed for a couple of hours because she looked shattered. While Chris was in bed, I sorted out the medication and dressings that she had been given on discharge from hospital. Quite a lot of stuff needed sorting. She had also been prescribed white knee-high elastic stockings to wear in order to prevent deep vein thrombosis in her legs post-surgery. It was my job to put them on for her in the morning and take them back off in the evening before she went to bed. My God, you have not done a workout until you have put a pair of those on someone.

Forget the gym membership, just buy a pair of surgical stockings and you will have the best workout ever. I was shattered by the time I had put them on her. There was obviously a knack to putting them on, but I never managed to work it out.

I was hoping that Chris would have a good sleep as she looked exhausted, but she got up about an hour later. She couldn't sleep. Perhaps she was overtired. I made us something to eat but Chris hardly touched hers, she wasn't hungry. She was quiet. I asked her if she was okay, she turned to me with a worried look and said, 'I'm scared.' I held her hand gently and reassured her that everything would be okay. It was only to be expected as she had been through a lot and had been looked after extremely well in hospital. Now she was back home, I think she felt that her security blanket had been taken away from her. The nurse at the hospital had told me that Chris would more than likely feel like this when she returned home. I tried my best to reassure her that I wouldn't let anything bad happen to her. I confirmed that someone would be with her at all times, and if there were any problems and I thought she needed medical attention, I would organise it for her.

I loved her and knew that we would get through this together. She was concerned about how she was going to manage when I needed to go food shopping. I reassured her by letting her know that Mum would be coming to sit with her and that everything would be fine. She seemed to be relieved when I had given her that information. There was no way I would have left her to fend for herself.

Days and weeks went on and things weren't good.

She developed a chest infection which she needed treatment for, and it appeared that no sooner was she getting over one chest infection, she would go straight on to get another. She also had problems with the scar on her leg where they had removed the vein. Part of the scar didn't appear to be healing properly and ended up turning into a Keloid scar, which meant that it had become raised and enlarged. The scar also reopened, so Chris had to go to the hospital again for treatment.

Weeks continued to pass, and it seemed as though she was getting no further forward. She wasn't recovering as well as we had hoped at home, and this impacted on her mood. She was low in herself and hitting out at people around her. One evening, we were watching TV, and suddenly she looked at me and said, 'Why are you still here?'

'What?' I asked, surprised.

'This is not what you signed up for!' she uttered, staring at me.

'Where has all this come from?' I asked.

'It's unfair that you should be having to look after me. You could find someone else, younger and fitter!'

'What's wrong, sweetheart?'

'I'm feeling particularly low today!' she replied, with tear-filled eyes.

I went and sat beside her on the sofa, took hold of her hand, and told her that I was exactly where I wanted to be. I reassured her that I loved her so much and that I would always be there for her. She reminded me that we couldn't be intimate, which of course was true. That side of the relationship had to be put on hold as Chris wasn't fit enough, but we knew this before she had surgery. We were both missing the intimate side of the relationship, but the recovery process couldn't be rushed. I emphasised that she was doing well, I was proud of her, and that she needed to be patient. She just needed some reassurance from me. I reminded her that she was my world, and that I was falling more and more in love with her every day. She needed to think positive, and before she knew it, everything would be back to normal.

Weeks went on, and Chris did start to pick up. The recurrent chest infections and problems she had encountered with the scar on her leg had had a significant impact on her recovery time, but finally she was starting to feel much better. She was self-conscious of the scars on her body, which she had acquired during surgery. They didn't bother me in the slightest, but I had to convince Chris of that. She started going out for short walks, and I think our first social outing post-surgery was to Mum's for Sunday lunch. When we got back home from Mum's, Chris was exhausted, so I suggested that she went to bed for a couple of hours.

She seemed to tire easily, and I felt that it was due to all that she had been through and the numerous problems she had encountered post-surgery. I went upstairs with her and decided to lie at the side of her for ten minutes, then I would go back downstairs as I had things to do. However, I fell asleep along with Chris and was woken up an hour later by her running her fingers through my hair. I looked at her and she said, 'You've fallen asleep.'

I smiled at her and said, 'I can't believe you have

just woken me up to tell me that I have fallen asleep.' At that point we both started laughing. I must have needed the sleep. She wasn't surprised at me falling asleep as I looked shattered, which she claimed was due to all the running around I had been doing while looking after her. She was concerned about how tired I was looking. I assured her that there was no need to worry about me, I was fine. She just needed to concentrate on getting better.

We were watching TV one evening when Chris announced that she fancied a night out, as we hadn't been out for weeks. I didn't think it was a good idea, but she insisted that it was something that she would like to do. I wondered if she felt up to it because we would be going into an environment that was likely to be extremely busy. I didn't want her getting pushed and shoved. She assured me that she would be okay. I wasn't too happy because I felt that it would end up being too much for Chris. I think I was still wrapping her in cotton wool to keep her safe at all times. However, she was keen to go, so I agreed as I just wanted her to be happy. An evening out would probably do her good, or so we thought!

We made arrangements to go to our usual venue in Sheffield on the Saturday evening. A family member gave us a lift there and collected us at the end of the evening. We were only going for a couple of hours, which I thought was long enough for Chris's first night out following her surgery. As soon as we walked into the pub, Sarah rushed up to us and gave us both a hug. She was thrilled to see us, asked Chris how she was doing, and we started chatting. I could see that Chris was enjoying herself as it was the first night out that we had had in a while, but I was still concerned about her. We sat at a table, and I was the one who kept going to the bar for drinks because I didn't want Chris getting jostled. Her chest was still tender from the surgery, and the last thing she needed was someone's elbow coming into contact with it. I was watching her like a hawk and thought to myself, *Am I being too overprotective here?* Then again, she was my partner, I loved her so much, and I didn't want any harm coming to her. We arrived back home around 11:30 pm and although we had enjoyed ourselves, I felt that the evening had been a bit of an endurance test for Chris. She looked shattered, so we went straight to bed.

The following morning, Mum phoned to ask if we had enjoyed our evening out. I revealed that we had but felt that it had been a bit too much for Chris. When she invited us for lunch, I said I would see what Chris wanted to do and get back to her. I mentioned it to Chris, and she stated that she wasn't hungry and didn't feel like going anywhere. I phoned Mum back and informed her that Chris didn't feel up to it and that we would probably call to see her during the week.

I came off the phone, looked at Chris and said, 'We need to talk.' I wanted to know what was wrong as it wasn't like her to refuse one of Mum's delicious Sunday roasts. She told me that she didn't feel hungry. 'Okay, now tell me the real reason,' I replied. She then admitted that she didn't want to go out and just wanted to have a quiet day at home with me, which of course I was happy to go along with. Although she had enjoyed going out the previous evening, it had been too much for her. I had a feeling it would be and was surprised when she had suggested going out. She now realised that it was a bit too soon to be having a night out and that she was obviously not fit enough to be socialising on that scale. She would have to gradually ease herself back into normality, and not rush things.

She had been to hell and back, what with one thing and another. Not only had she gone through the surgery, but she had also had to cope with all the setbacks since she returned home. Chris started to get upset and said, 'You won't ever leave me, will you?' I reminded her how much I loved her and that I would never leave her. She suggested that I ignore her as she was having a bad day. I thought she was picking up, but it now seemed as though she was going backwards, and I felt that she was trying to run before she could walk. I made her a coffee, we carried on talking, and I suggested that we went for a leisurely walk as it was a nice day. She didn't want to leave the house. The choice was hers, and if she didn't want to go, it was fine. She asked me if I would still be going for a walk, and I assured her that I wouldn't go without her. She hoped that would be my answer as she didn't want me to leave her. I made us both some lunch, and although Chris wasn't supposed to be hungry, she ate most of it.

After lunch I suggested that Chris went to have a lie down as she looked tired. She asked me what I would be doing while she was in bed, and I informed her that I was going to do some writing. She said, 'You're not going out, are you?' I reassured her that I wouldn't be going anywhere, and that I wouldn't leave her in the house on her own. I would be downstairs, and she could shout me if she needed anything. She went to bed, I got on with some writing and managed to get quite a bit done.

I couldn't understand what was wrong. Chris was very clingy, and she never wanted me to be far away from her. She was a strong person, and always seemed to handle everything that life threw at her, but at that time it appeared that she needed lots of reassurance from me, which of course I was more than happy to give her. I needed to keep telling her that everything was going to be okay, and that things would soon return to normal.

When she got up around 4 pm, she seemed a bit brighter in herself. She had a shower, and I made her a coffee. While we were chatting, I asked her how she was feeling. She felt better as she had had a good sleep. She suggested going to see Mum the following day. As it was her suggestion, I knew that she must feel up to going. I phoned Mum and asked her if it was okay to visit the following day, and of course it was. Mum offered to cook Sunday lunch on Monday, as she hadn't bothered cooking it because she was on her own.

The following day, as planned, we went to Mum's, and we had a lovely day. We had a beautiful lunch, and Chris seemed to be relaxed; it was good to see her being less tense. We told Mum that we wanted to take her out for a nice meal at some point to say thank you for all her help while Chris had been recovering. She had been there for us from the minute Chris became ill. She would sit with Chris if I had to go into town and would also get us bits of shopping if we needed it. She was a diamond, and we couldn't thank her enough for what she had done. She was the one person we could always rely on. She was happy to go out for a meal, so we arranged it for the following day. We arrived back home from Mum's early evening and Chris was tired, as usual, so she had a shower and went to bed early. It was too early for me to go to bed, so I stayed up and listened to some music.

The following morning, Chris revealed that she had slept well, and that she felt good in herself. It was music to my ears. As promised, we took Mum out for a nice meal and also bought her a lovely bunch of flowers and some chocolates to say, 'Thank you.' She had always been good to us, right from the moment I told her that Chris and I were together. She was always there for us, with a listening ear, and to offer advice if either of us ever needed it. We took Mum to a nice pub and had a lovely meal, and then went back to her house for a couple of hours. It was nice just to sit and unwind and chat. I thought that Chris looked good in herself, better than she had done for a while, and Mum remarked on it too.

A couple of weeks passed, and Chris was feeling the benefit of having had heart surgery. She felt fitter and was now able to do things which she had been unable to do prior to surgery. She could walk further, and she was able to potter around in the garden, which was something she enjoyed. It was lovely that she was now free from chest pain and breathlessness, and we were both confident that her quality of life would now be vastly improved, physically and emotionally. She was going out more, and just generally getting her life back on track. It was the best that she had felt in a long while.

I was thrilled because at last she was getting back to her old self. I loved her so much, and it had been an emotional time for both of us as she had been unwell for such a long time. It had been a long road to recovery, but finally she had got there, and everything was getting back to normal.

CHAPTER 22

Birthday Celebrations and Sadness

I t was 1997, and Chris was going to be celebrating her fiftieth birthday in the middle of the year, so I wanted to do something special for her. Initially, she wasn't sure what she wanted to do to celebrate her birthday, though we had discussed the possibility of having a party. I also wanted to take her out for a nice meal. Certain other family members had the same idea, but they wanted to take her for the meal on the day of her birthday, just as I did. Chris made it clear that she would be more than happy to eat out with family members the day before or the day after her birthday, because she wanted to have her birthday meal with me on the actual day and did not wish to go out for two meals on the same day. However, that didn't suit certain family members, and they weren't prepared to take her out for a meal on an alternative day. They wouldn't budge.

I asked Chris what she would like to do. After all, it was going to be her day, and the decision was entirely hers. 'More than anything else, I would love to have a party at the gay pub,' she said. I was quite surprised because a party had been mentioned earlier in the year, but nothing more had been said on the matter. I thought it was a great idea. All I wanted was for Chris to be happy and enjoy her special day. If she was happy, then I was happy.

We talked it over, and Chris had her heart set on having a birthday party. We had a word with the landlord, and he was delighted that we would be celebrating Chris's birthday there. We got on well with him, so we knew that he would be willing to accommodate us. We now had a party to plan, which involved inviting guests, sorting out food, and all things party related. We had a few weeks to organise everything, or should I say I had a few weeks to organise the party, as Chris was never that keen on organising events. She normally left that side of things to me, which I was more than happy to do. She would organise something if she had to, she was more than capable, but she always preferred me to take the lead when anything needed to be organised.

We had decided to do our own catering, with Mum's help of course. Everything was coming together, and the day of Chris's fiftieth birthday arrived. I had bought her a gold chain, along with a few other presents. The party was also my gift to her. I took Chris out for her birthday meal at lunchtime and once we were back home, it was time to start preparing the food and getting everything organised for the evening. It was all hands on deck as there was plenty to prepare, and it also needed transporting to the venue and setting out, which the landlord helped with. We always preferred to do our own catering. That way you know exactly what you are eating, the surroundings the food has been prepared in, and the cleanliness of the people preparing it. Both Chris and I were particular when it came to all things food related.

Certain members of Chris's family declined the invitation to the party because they hadn't got their own way regarding taking Chris out for a meal. I think it was a matter of, 'I couldn't take you for a meal when I wanted to, so I'm not going to your party.' Teddy and pram spring to mind!

Chris had invited her sister, Janet, as it was the correct thing to do, that way she couldn't say that she had been left out. Chris pointed out to her that the evening was going to be held at a gay venue, and we automatically assumed that she would decline the invitation as she didn't approve of the relationship Chris and I had, and we both thought that there was no way she would want to spend the evening in a gay pub. However, Janet surprised us both by accepting the invitation. I was gutted! I honestly could not for the life of me think why she would want to be a part of the celebrations when she was so against Chris and I being together. She didn't want to miss her sister's fiftieth birthday party, or so we thought!

A lot of our friends at that time were people who used to go into the pub, so we had invited them. They went in most weeks, so we knew that they would be there anyway. Before we knew it, it was almost time for the party to begin. Chris, Mum and I arrived early and some of our friends were already in the pub, and the rest of our friends turned up shortly after us.

Janet appeared around an hour later, with another family member. I think that it was more than likely curiosity on her part in the way that she probably wanted to see what it was like in a gay pub. I feel that her intentions were to sit there with a look of disgust on her face all evening as that is exactly what she did. She hardly spoke to me and didn't have that much to say to Chris. Trying to have a conversation with her was like pulling teeth, and you get to the point where you just stop trying.

Chris and I were dancing and having a good time; it was Chris's night and all I wanted was for her to enjoy the evening. Mum was enjoying the party, chatting with some of our friends and getting on well with them, yet Janet had a face on her that would have turned milk sour. However, Chris was enjoying herself and that was all that mattered to me. We had both had quite a bit to drink as friends were buying birthday drinks for Chris, and drinks for me as well. We weren't drunk, shall I say we were merry. The majority of the time we paced ourselves when we were drinking to avoid the result of being drunk, but there will always be the odd time when you have that extra drink and regret it the following day. There is nothing worse than having too much to drink, getting back home, walking into the bedroom which appears to be spinning and saying, 'The next time that bed comes around, I'm getting on it.' I would imagine that most of us have done it at some point!

Towards the end of the evening, slow songs were being played. Chris took hold of my hand, and we went onto the dance floor for a smooch. As we were dancing, I looked over Chris's shoulder at Janet, and her face had a look of disgust all over it. She knew she would be spending the evening at a gay venue, and this was one of the things that she should have expected to see. We both noticed that she was looking at us intermittently, and Chris purposely waited until she was looking and at that point, she kissed me. Janet's face was like thunder, but Mum was looking at us and smiling. I think Mum knew that Chris had kissed me to prove a point. The dance ended, and we went back to our table, at which point Chris's sister got her things together and informed us that she was leaving. Chris walked to the door with her and off she went. It appeared that her purpose for that evening was to be as unsociable as she could be, and I feel that she had set out to ruin the evening for Chris. However, it hadn't worked as Chris had had a lovely evening and she was so happy. We were in such a good place; we were enjoying life and all that it had to offer!

A few days passed, and Chris decided to go and see Janet to find out why she had acted the way she had at the party. I didn't go with her as I felt that it was a sister thing, and they needed to sort it out on their own. Chris asked her why she had been so unsociable, which didn't go down well. Janet told Chris not to go down the road of questioning her and that she should be grateful that she went to the party in the first place. Chris explained that she felt as though she had gone with the purpose of trying to spoil the evening. Her sister's reply to that was, 'Well, I certainly didn't enjoy myself.' She informed Chris that she had felt uncomfortable being in that type of environment.

Chris said, 'What did you expect? You were going into a gay pub!' Chris said that she would have understood if she had declined the invitation, but what she couldn't understand was the fact that she had gone when she was so against gay people and gay pubs.

Janet then stated that she had gone because she wanted to be a part of Chris's birthday celebrations and felt that it was the right thing to do. She then went on to say that she was curious and wanted to see what it was like in one of the pubs where *'you lot'* hang out. Chris said, 'What do you mean, *'you lot'?'* By this time Chris was starting to feel annoyed by some of the things that Janet was saying so she decided to leave. Following that conversation, Chris and her sister weren't on the best of terms, and there was minimal contact between them. Weeks went on, and there seemed to be no improvement in Janet's attitude towards our relationship.

They were once close, but Chris felt that the way her sister was reacting was driving a wedge between them. In theory, she should have been pleased that Chris was now in a relationship with someone who loved her very much and was loyal, as Chris had also been in a bad marriage many years before we got together. However, she just could not accept the fact that Chris's partner was a woman. It wasn't me as a person that she didn't like, it was the fact that I was Chris's female partner that she couldn't come to terms with. She was the type of person that outsiders couldn't get close to, and there always seemed to be a line that you couldn't cross with her. She would give Chris a hug, but she would never give me a hug, which to be honest didn't bother me at all.

All things considered, by this time Chris and I had already been together for quite a few years, so her sister had had more than enough time to get used to the fact that Chris was gay. From the word go, she was against us being together and described our relationship as being a 'phase' we were going through, and that it would be a 'flash in the pan' and would never last. It would have been nice if she could have accepted it and supported us, but sadly it wasn't to be.

You never knew where you stood with her. Don't get me wrong, you could have a laugh with her, when she was in a sociable mood, but then at other times, she would have little to say to you. I always found her to be hard work to be honest, which was a shame because she was Chris's sister and I so wanted things to be different between us, but they never were. She certainly never welcomed me into the family with open arms.

One time when Chris and I called at her sister's, she was quite offhand with both of us. Maybe she was just having a bad day, I don't know, but if she was, she shouldn't have taken it out on us. She criticised both me and Chris and revealed that she couldn't understand why two women would want to be in a relationship with each other. She admitted that she would never feel totally comfortable around people who were in a same-sex relationship. Things were said that maybe shouldn't have been, on both sides, as is often the case when a conversation gets heated, and at that point we left.

Chris and Janet didn't have any contact with each other for a long time following that heated discussion as Chris wasn't prepared to tolerate that type of behaviour. All correspondence stopped, as did birthday cards, Christmas cards, phone calls and so on, for quite some time. Then, all of a sudden Janet made contact because she thought things needed sorting out, between all of us. We arranged a time and place to meet, and we talked, or should I say Chris and her sister did the majority of the talking, I was mainly observing. Chris pointed out that Janet had been out of order, and she agreed. Chris informed her that our relationship was for keeps, it wasn't going away, and that it was something she needed to deal with. If she was unable to deal with it, she should at least keep her opinions to herself, because we didn't want to hear them. Janet then assured Chris that she would try to be a bit more understanding of our relationship. Chris pointed out that things had been said in the past that were hurtful and unnecessary and felt that her sister owed me an apology. She agreed and did apologise to me. I accepted it but inside I was thinking, *I bet it has nearly choked you trying to get those words of apology out to me.*

Things had been sorted, and we were all on speaking terms once again. I felt sorry for Chris as all she wanted was for her sister to accept our relationship and to be happy for us, but sadly it didn't happen, she never fully accepted it. I can remember Chris telling me right at the start of our relationship that her sister would have a problem dealing with us being together, and she wasn't wrong. Everything appeared to be fine following the conversation and the apology, though there were still occasions when Chris and Janet would go for long periods without speaking. Their relationship had changed, and Chris always felt that things were never the same between them, which upset Chris as they used to be close. However, Chris was resigned to the situation. She'd tried her best. As the saying goes, you can choose your friends, but you can't choose your family!

CHAPTER 23

Moving Home

Months went on, and not only were members of Chris's family making life difficult for us, but we also had to tolerate the many unwanted remarks from our homophobic neighbours. They used chat to us, and we would have a laugh and a joke with them, then suddenly the tide turned, and it was as though they wanted to do everything they possibly could to make life uncomfortable for us. This had continued for a couple of years. One or two other people on the street also used to make pathetic comments and gestures towards Chris and I regarding our sexuality. All the usual ones that you expect to hear from small-minded people when you are gay. We got to the point where we could not put up with this childish behaviour anymore, and we had a discussion about moving.

We were currently living in a three-bedroom house with large front and rear gardens, which I might add were becoming too much for us to tend. We decided to look for an alternative property in a completely different area, so we went into the Council Lettings Office to enquire about an exchange. We looked through the many lists of properties, trying to find something that would suit our needs. At that time, this was what you did, whereas now I believe that it's all done online. To our surprise, there was someone wanting to exchange their home for one in the area where we were living, but their property was only a two-bedroom flat, which was on the first floor. However, we contacted the tenants and made arrangements to view their property.

It was in a much better area than where we were currently living, and we were excited to think that this could potentially be our new home, if everything went well. We drove down a quiet, tree-lined street, looking for the property. We arrived at a two-storey block of flats that looked neat and tidy on the outside. Our first impression was good. We were greeted by the tenants and shown around. We were impressed, in fact we fell in love with the flat on the first viewing. It was a good-sized property, close to amenities, and in a secure building, which was ideal. However, it was a flat, not a house, which meant that we would be losing a bedroom and our gardens. So not only would we be downsizing, but we would also be losing our much-loved private outdoor space. Is this what we really wanted to do? We were initially unsure!

When we returned home that evening, we had a long chat about the flat. We wondered if we would be making a mistake moving from our spacious three-bedroom house to a smaller two-bedroom flat. However, it was a lovely property, and after weighing up all the pros and cons, we decided that it would be big enough for our requirements. The tenants, who were a couple with a young child, had mentioned they were looking for an alternative property with a garden. They thought our house would suit them perfectly, so we arranged for them to come and view our property. I kept saying to Chris, 'What if they don't like our house? We won't be able to move!' She pointed out that we would just have to wait and see how things went and hope that their response to our property would be favourable.

The day arrived for them to view our property, and we couldn't settle. We so wanted them to like our house and for it to be suitable for them as a family. However, we needn't have worried as they loved everything about it. They were instantly impressed with the house. The large lawned garden at the rear was a bonus and would be ideal for their small child. We would be leaving them a good shed, lawnmower and other garden tools that we would no longer have a use for. Before they left, we made a mutual decision that we would start the ball rolling with the relevant authorities in order to exchange properties.

Before the exchange could be approved, we had to have a home visit from the housing officer. This was arranged, the visit went well, the exchange was approved, and we had to wait several weeks for everything to go through. We couldn't wait to tell Mum and take her to see our new home. She was pleased for us and loved the flat just as much as we did. This was an exciting time for us, as we would finally be saying goodbye to the street where we had encountered a lot of problems from small-minded people because of our sexuality. Everything was going along nicely, and we started packing things ready for moving. We had been informed that the exchange would be going through and that it was just a matter of agreeing a moving date.

We started to take a few boxes and small items up to the flat, and the couple brought some of their belongings to our home to store. That way, there would be fewer items to transport on the actual moving day. We were getting impatient as the day for moving didn't appear to be coming fast enough. I was starting to wonder if the other couple had backed out and decided that they didn't want to exchange after all. I was desperate to move, and I informed Chris that if the exchange fell through, I wasn't unpacking my things. She looked at me with a puzzled look on her face, and I said, 'I can't stay here, Chris.'

She then said, 'If you go, I'm coming with you.'

It had been an agonising wait, but at last we were notified of the date when our tenancy at the new property would commence. Feeling elated and relieved, we danced around the lounge and hugged each other.

Finally, moving day arrived, and we were off to our new home. This was to be a long, tiring day. The couple we were exchanging with had borrowed a van for the weekend, and they, along with a couple of other people, manoeuvred our furniture into our new home. It took longer than it should have because everything had to be carried up a flight of stairs. I was thirty-six when we moved into the property, so the stairs weren't an issue. I could run up and down them whilst carrying boxes, bedside tables, suitcases, and other items.

Everything was upside down, as you would expect, and we didn't know where to begin. We moved in four weeks before Christmas, so time wasn't on our side; we wanted everything to be organised by then. We had lots to do, so over the next couple of weeks we cracked on and got as much done as we possibly could, and Mum did as much as she could to help. Chris and I were so excited about this new chapter in our lives. Plus, it was going to be a fresh start in a property where we would now be joint tenants. Things were changing and we were looking forward to life in our new home.

We enjoyed celebrating our first Christmas in our new home. It was exciting, decorating our tree and setting out Christmas ornaments, while having a glass of wine and singing along to Christmas songs playing in the background. We went to Mum's on Christmas Day for lunch, and Mum came to us for Boxing Day lunch. This was what we usually did every year. We had a lovely time. The attitude of the immediate neighbours was completely different to what we had been experiencing in our previous property. They were friendly and always had a kind word for me and Chris. Chris and I knew that we were going to be happy here.

A couple of years after we had moved into our flat, a property became available next door to us. I made a passing comment to Mum about it, and she said that it would suit her. I asked her if she was serious, and she confirmed that she was. She had recently lost her dog due to him having fits, so she was rattling around in a three-bedroom house on her own. Also, she had no central heating upstairs which made it extremely cold during the winter months, which wasn't good for Mum as she had angina, and suffered with bronchitis. Mum wondered how we would feel if she moved next door to us, and we told her that it would be great and that we would love it if we were all living in close proximity. She asked me to make some enquiries about the property and find out what her chances were of being offered it. The following day, I contacted the relevant people to make enquiries on Mum's behalf. I was advised that there was a waiting list for all the properties, but they would look into it and let us know if they had anyone lined up for that flat.

The same day, I received a phone call from the person I had previously spoken to regarding the vacant property, and they informed me that although it was normal practice to go onto the waiting list, no one on the list was waiting for a first-floor property at that time. I asked if that meant that Mum would be offered the property, and I was told that there was a good chance. Prior to that, they would need to do a home visit and talk to Mum. Arrangements were made for the housing officer to visit Mum and fill out the necessary paperwork. As Mum had already been led to believe that there was a good chance she would be offered the property, she had started packing a few things. I appreciate that we were probably getting a bit ahead of ourselves, but we felt that it was more or less in the bag.

We were at Mum's when the housing officer arrived. She was lovely, and Chris and I always got on well with her. She had a good chat with Mum and was eager to know why she wanted to move home. Mum explained the reasons why. She was living on her own in a large, cold house in an area which was rapidly going downhill and needed a smaller property in a better area, and she wanted to be close to me and Chris because of health reasons. I informed the housing officer that I had been led to believe that the property would be offered to Mum, and she had started doing a little bit of packing.

She looked at me, smiled, and said that her visit that day was just a formality and to continue packing. She did, however, state that Mum would be informed in writing within the next few days. A couple of days later Mum received a letter officially offering her the property next door to us. We were so excited.

We had to get stuck in and help Mum to get everything in the house packed up ready for moving. We hired a large van, which Chris drove. Moving day arrived, and we were all up early, ready to make a start. We had stayed at Mum's the previous night as we felt that it would be more practical to do so. There were numerous trips to make, and one of our neighbours kindly helped with the heavy lifting. Finally, all of Mum's things had been transported and she was in her new home. Everything was upside down, as you would expect, but she was only next door to us now, so we were on hand 24/7 to help get things sorted out in the property. It had been a long day and we were all shattered, but we still needed to get Mum's bed made and unpack various other items for the flat to be habitable that night.

The following day, the hard work started, and continued for several days to come. We all got stuck in and put everything into place in Mum's new home. It seemed strange having Mum living next door and not having to travel several miles to visit her. It was lovely having her so close to us, and it meant that we could keep an eye on her and always make sure she was safe. We were good friends with Paul, the neighbour who had helped us when Mum moved in. He was always on hand if we needed anything moving that was heavy. He knew that Chris and I were a couple, and it was lovely to have a neighbour who didn't judge us or make any un-wanted comments regarding our sexuality. We used to occasionally go to his flat in the evening to spend a bit of time with him, as he never had any company. We always used to have a laugh and he loved it. He used to say that I came out with some great one-liners. He wasn't in a good position financially because he wasn't working at that time, so we used to make him the odd meal and nearly always a Sunday lunch.

When Christmas came around, Paul was unable to buy much extra food for the festive period as his finances wouldn't allow him to. We wanted to make sure that he had a good Christmas, so we made a couple of hampers up for him. One hamper contained food cupboard items, mince pies, Christmas cake, choc-olates, ham, pickles, and all those sorts of things, while the other hamper was filled with fruit, vegetables, and salad items. He was overjoyed when we gave them to him because he had not managed to get much in him-self. We did this each year for him, so he always had a pretty good idea what his Christmas present from us would be. We always made sure he had a good Christ-mas Day and Boxing Day lunch too.

He was a good friend and neighbour, but unfor-tunately, he passed away suddenly. We were devastated. His sister, Lynda, had previously lived in South York-shire but had emigrated to New Zealand, and still lives there. She had to make arrangements to fly over to Eng-land to sort her brother's affairs out and organise his funeral, which all took time. Rather than her having to incur extra costs from booking into a hotel, we invited her to stay with us for the duration of her visit. We had met her once in the past and got on well with her. We were looking forward to seeing her again, although it would be due to sad circumstances.

Lynda is a lovely, easy-going person, with a good sense of humour, and we all became good friends. She reminisced about her brother, and we expressed how it had been a privilege to have known him. She also revealed what life was like living in New Zealand, and how certain things had different names from what they were called in England. She told us that fish and chips are known as a Maori roast in New Zealand, and they don't have mushy peas, scraps, or vinegar. Sweets are called lollies, and ice lollies are known as ice blocks. It was interesting hearing what life was like living out there.

We made the most of the time while she was staying with us, by way of days out, and a trip to the coast. I'm pretty sure that the trip to Bridlington will have stuck in Lynda's mind. It took long enough to get there. At that time, there were a few diversions in place due to roadworks, and for some reason we kept getting lost and ended up miles from where we should have been. Though we all found it funny, Chris was getting frustrated because she was unable to get onto the correct road that would take us to Bridlington. We did eventually arrive at our destination, many hours after we had left home. It was something we laughed about, for many years.

Although Lynda stayed with us for three weeks, the time just flew, and before we knew it, she was packing her case to return home. We had had so many laughs while she was with us and enjoyed spending time with her. There were lots of hugs and tears on the day that she left, and she gave us an open invitation to visit her in New Zealand, and of course, she would always be welcome to come and stay with us. We speak occasionally on the phone, which sometimes takes a bit of working out, due to the time difference. She may be thousands of miles away, but she's a good friend and she will always hold a special place in my heart.

CHAPTER 24

Lifestyle Changes

W hat's happening? I thought as I stood in front of the lift door at my local hospital. I could feel myself becoming anxious at the thought of getting in. Finally, the long-awaited lift arrived, and the doors dinged open. A stream of people rushed out and went on their way. I had travelled in lifts many times before, so I just couldn't understand why this time should be any different. But it was different, something had changed. I froze, my body was rigid with fear, and I could not get in. I turned and walked away with tears in my eyes. I could not believe what had just happened! Was it just a one-off or was this something which was likely to occur again? I was filled with frustration; this metal box had beaten me.

Days and weeks went by, and I kept my distance from anywhere that meant going in a lift would be likely, but I needed to try and fight this. I could not let it beat me. I decided to try again and hopefully master it this time. Who was I fooling? The same thing happened again, and again. I can't keep putting myself through this, I thought, so I won't even try anymore. I'll use the stairs; it will be fine.

Months turned into years, and I battled on with my phobia of lifts. As I have a fear of confined spaces, the thought of a lift breaking down with me inside fills me with dread. Lifts do, on occasion, break down, and I have convinced myself that whatever lift I get into is going to be the one that breaks down, and I will be stuck in it. I understand there is a 'will it, won't it' way of looking at life, but I always assume that it will.

It was as though one thing followed another, and another, as I realised when I boarded a train to go and visit a friend in a Sheffield hospital. I started to feel uncomfortable and was almost at the point of getting off the train. I should have stepped straight off, but I dithered about too much and missed my opportunity. The doors closed, and the train set off. My heart started pounding. Sweat trickled down my forehead. Nausea rose from the pit of my stomach. I was shaking. I needed to get off the train, but you can't just ring the bell like you can on a bus. I felt trapped and was getting to the point where I thought I would be forced to pull the emergency stop cord. A kind lady noticed that I looked distressed and came over to me. I told her that I needed to get off the train as I was having a panic attack. She informed me that we weren't far from the first stop, and I would be able to leave the train there. It took roughly seven minutes to reach that stop but to me it seemed like the longest train journey on God's earth.

I could not comprehend why this was happening! My life was changing, and I felt that I was being forced into a new life of fear and uncertainty. Years went on and nothing appeared to change for me. My panic disorder remained the same, and it was something that I was learning to live with. I steered clear of any situation where my comfort would be compromised. It was difficult for me as I now felt that I was missing out on certain things. My mum and Chris always supported me and listened to me without judgement. They knew my limitations and what I would feel uncomfortable with. They understood.

If the fear of lifts and trains wasn't enough, I also developed a fear of motorways. My fear is being stuck in slow-moving traffic or traffic which is at a standstill. I tried to make sense of this and when I sat and thought about it, I could understand the reasoning behind it. If I were a passenger in a car on a normal road and the traffic wasn't moving, I would have the option of getting out if I wanted to, therefore I would be in control of my actions. However, on the motorway, you are restricted in the way that you are unable to just get out of your car and wander about. Therefore, if there were a tailback of traffic on the motorway, the feeling of being trapped would envelop me.

I would imagine that this may seem a little odd to someone who doesn't suffer with phobias and anxiety, but for the affected, like myself, it is very concerning. I was starting to build a picture in my mind of why these kinds of situations were having such an impact on my life. The reason became clear to me, and I felt that it was due to being in situations where I'm not in control. Remember what I said about ringing the bell to get off the bus if I felt uncomfortable, that is me being in control. But on the train, I was unable to ring the bell and get off, so that is me not being in control. It sounds strange, I know, but it was all beginning to make sense to me.

I used to feel safe when I was out with Chris and Mum, but when out on my own I felt vulnerable. This was getting out of hand to the point where I feared going anywhere on my own. Things had to change - and I made sure that they did! I used to make a point of going out somewhere on my own at least one day each week, either to the local town or to a shopping outlet. That seemed to go quite well, as I was in control of where I went and what time I returned home. I felt fine in the shops, even if they were busy, because I knew I could walk out at any point if I felt uncomfortable, which meant that I was in control.

One day, in the medical imaging department at my local hospital, I heard an announcement stating that the fire alarm was going to be tested. I thought, *That's fine, nothing to worry about.* I waited, and the fire alarm sounded, but along with the alarm going off, all the fire doors automatically closed. My pulse raced, and my hands started to become sweaty. I felt trapped and anxious as I was unsure of how long the doors would remain closed. Luckily, they were only closed for less than a minute, so I was fine. I kept thinking to myself that this was ridiculous. Yes, the doors had closed automatically, but it wasn't the same as being trapped in a lift, it was a spacious area with windows and there were people around. There had been no real reason for me to get into a panic, therefore I needed to address this. No one else had appeared to be bothered about the alarm sounding and the doors closing. However, I do feel that the staff should have stated that the fire doors would automatically close in order to give people the opportunity to leave the room if they wanted to.

I often feel frustrated with how people perceive panic disorder. I have in the past had to attend appointments that have been several floors up in a building which I have had to access via the stairs. On mentioning this to a member of staff, they have stated that the lifts are quick, and it doesn't take long between floors. I have pointed out to them that I am unable to use the lift due to anxiety and the fear of being trapped in one. They have said that I wouldn't be in the lift long, only a few seconds. *Oh, well that's alright then,* I used to think to myself, *because a lift couldn't possibly break down in a few seconds.*

People have also suggested that I would probably be okay in a glass lift because I would be able to see out, but unfortunately that wouldn't make any difference whatsoever. I would still be trapped if the lift broke down. I wish people would accept it when I tell them I am unable to use a lift instead of trying to persuade me to. Do people think I would rather climb up five or six flights of stairs than use a lift? It is very frustrating for me when I have to walk past a lift and start climbing stairs.

I suppose for someone to fully understand how a person with panic disorder feels, they would have to experience it themselves. I appreciate that they are just trying to help and make life easier for me, but I don't think they realise how they are adding to my anxiety when they are trying to encourage me to do something that I know I would be unable to do. One thing I don't appreciate is people raising their voice, which has happened, when questioning why I am unable to do something. When I tell someone I am unable to do something, that should be an end to it. I shouldn't be made to feel inadequate or be pressured into doing something which is beyond my comfort zone. This is who I am, and if people are unable to accept that, they know what the alternative is.

If I go into a pub or a café and it is quite crowded, surprisingly I feel okay, as long as I'm not too far away from the door. The volume of people doesn't affect me to a great extent, as I don't have to interact with them. What does bother me, is being out with a large group of people all sitting at the same table, because then I would have to interact with them all, which I would find challenging. I'm more than happy to go out for the evening with friends, as long as the party only consists of maybe six people.

It is extremely difficult to live your life with phobias and the constant fear of being subjected to a situation where a panic attack is likely. Some people may think, just get a grip, you'll be fine, but it doesn't work that way. Unless you have been in a situation where your heart begins to race, your head starts spinning and you start sweating, then I'm sorry but you can't possibly know how a person feels when they are experiencing an attack. This isn't just something that happens to you one day, and then it's gone the next. This is a medical condition that many people suffer with on a daily basis, and it's not to be ridiculed.

I feel embarrassed when I have to explain to people why I am unable to do certain things. I would be delighted to be able to do all the things that other people do and live a normal life - but sadly I can't. I envy people who can happily go about their day-to-day business knowing that everything is going to be fine. For me, that isn't the case as I am constantly wondering whether I am going to be subjected to a situation where I am likely to suffer a panic attack.

It isn't a good way for someone to be living their life because it impacts on so many normal things that most people take for granted. There are places that I know I am unable to visit, because they are either too far away from home, or they are likely to cause me too much anxiety. So, I stay at home, where I feel safe. If you have never suffered a panic attack, and don't have any phobias, think yourselves very lucky, and enjoy every moment of your life while you can. One day, everything could change, and you could find yourself in my shoes.

I can remember a time when I was able to use a lift, and travel on a train, but these days, it just would not happen. I have spent years trying to overcome these phobias, with no success. It bothers me a great deal as I feel that I am missing out on so much in life. But in a way I suppose I have got used to it because this is now how I live my life. I don't know what triggered these phobias about different things, but I would like to be optimistic and think that one day my life will change to the extent that I am able to live a normal life once again. I live in hope!

CHAPTER 25

Back to School

I n 2004, Chris and I enrolled on a course at the college in our local town. It appeared that if we didn't familiarise ourselves with the world of computers, we were in danger of being left behind in an ever-changing world. On the first day, we arrived at college for our two-hour session which would take place weekly. We patiently waited outside the classroom, feeling excited and eager for the session to begin. We were joined by a few others who had also enrolled, which made up a class of approximately ten students. Some of the students were around my age, and others were closer to Chris's age. They were friendly, and we were all chatting while waiting outside the classroom. The tutor arrived and we all went in, which seemed rather strange as I had not been in a classroom for twenty-eight years, and it was even longer for Chris.

It looked different from how I remembered a classroom. There were two rows of long desks with computers placed on them at intervals. We were left to choose where we wanted to sit, and that would be our place of work for the duration of the course. I noticed that there was a whiteboard on the wall, which had replaced the blackboard I was more familiar with when I was at school.

The tutor introduced herself and asked each one of us to stand up and introduce ourselves and say a little bit about why we had enrolled on the course. This didn't go down well with me as I'm not a fan of public speaking, even in small groups. However, I managed to say a few words, but was eager to return to my seat. Chris didn't do much better than me, because she wasn't a fan of public speaking either. The tutor did a lot of talking in our first two-hour lesson as she was explaining different things relating to operating a computer. We then familiarised ourselves with the keyboard, screen and different programs. I was already familiar with some aspects because I had done typing at school as one of my subjects. I had also briefly used a computer in the past. Chris had never used a computer before, so everything was completely new to her.

In what seemed like no time at all, the lesson had come to an end. We left the room armed with copious amounts of literature relating to what had been discussed during the lesson. We were asked to have a look through the information at home before the next lesson. We had enjoyed it; the tutor was lovely and the other students in the class were friendly.

We were advised that in addition to the computer course, we would also be allowed to use the computers in the college library, free of charge in our own time if we chose to. This was brilliant as we could use the library to practise assignments ready for the following week.

One of our friends seemed confident that, in

time, we would end up purchasing a computer of our own, so we were able to practise at home. We both told him that there was no way we would be buying a computer, as it would be an unnecessary expense when we were able to use the facilities in the college library on a regular basis. However, time went on and we did end up buying a computer, desk, chair, and printer. Yes, we got the job lot!

This meant that the corner of our lounge had now turned into a classroom. So much for saying that we definitely wouldn't be buying! This worked out great as it meant that we could both get plenty of practice at home, without having to trail to the college library in all weathers.

We were both thoroughly enjoying the course and learning such a lot about the world of computers, so much so that two hours a week didn't seem long enough. As the lesson ended each week, I was longing for the following week to arrive, so we were able to get back to college. I loved the relaxed atmosphere in the classroom, and the tutor was extremely knowledgeable. She had an abundance of patience, which she needed, because not all the students were learning at the same pace. Each week, we would start an exercise from one of the books we had been given, but we were always advised to familiarise ourselves with the next few exercises before the following week's lesson. Chris and I always used to practise at home, so we were able to get straight on with the work at college the following week. We were coming on in leaps and bounds and were ready to start the next book before some of the others in the class. This was mainly due to the amount of practice we were doing at home, in our own time.

Eventually, the course came to an end, and we were both eager to sign up for the following class which would take us to the next level of computing. The new course was slightly more advanced, as you would expect, but we were still enjoying our weekly class at college and wanted to extend our knowledge of computers.

We enrolled for the next level, but at that time we were having extensive refurbishment work done on our property, and it was debatable whether we would be able to continue with the course. We managed to attend a couple of classes, but we then had to withdraw as the refurbishment works were turning into a nightmare. Since the computer class was only for three hours, one morning a week, we had assumed that we would be able to juggle the class along with the refurbishment works. However, it didn't work out as planned. We were both needed at home permanently in order to oversee each phase of the renovation, which meant that we were unable to devote any time to college. Consequently, we had to withdraw from the course, which meant that we failed to complete that level. We were both extremely disappointed.

Unfortunately, we never returned to college. We did, however, both obtain level one and level two National Open College Network certificates in Information and Communications Technology, which we were both thrilled about, and proud to receive.

CHAPTER 26

Mum's Seventieth Birthday

I n 2009, Mum was to celebrate her seventieth birthday, and Chris and I wanted to do something special for her. Had her birthday been in the summer months we would have taken her on holiday, but since her birthday was in January, going on holiday wasn't an option, especially in this country as it would have been too cold. Chris and I talked at length and decided to organise a surprise birthday party for Mum. At first, we were in two minds whether it would be a good idea because her birthday was in the middle of winter, and we did have reservations regarding the weather. We both thought that it would just be our luck to organise a party then not be able to get to the venue due to heavy snow. It wasn't common for us to have heavy snow in the winter, but knowing our luck, this would be the year that we got a thick covering. However, it was a risk we were prepared to take. We just thought what will be, will be.

It took quite a bit of organising, especially with Mum living next door to us, but it was a pleasure to be planning such a lovely event for a special lady. There were lots of things to arrange: a venue, music, and food.

We sent invitations out to a multitude of people: old friends Mum hadn't seen in years, friends of mine that neither of us had seen in years, and neighbours who we saw most days, and awaited replies. Once we had a rough idea of how many would be attending, we were able to do some costing regarding food as we would be self-catering.

As Mum's birthday was a couple of weeks after Christmas, it would have been foolish not to take advantage of some of the party food offers that are available in the supermarkets during the run-up to Christmas and New Year. However, along with all the usual fare that one buys for Christmas, we wondered how we could possibly manage to find room to store it in our freezer. It was too good an opportunity to miss so we bought some food and just hoped that we would be able to accommodate it.

We had the idea that whatever we couldn't fit in our freezer would hopefully find a short home in someone else's freezer. But then we thought, *Who on God's earth has spare room in their freezer at Christmas? No one!* It was no good asking Mum if she had room in her freezer as the food was for her party, and we didn't want her becoming suspicious. I repositioned quite a lot of things in our freezer and managed to get the extra food in although it wasn't in any kind of order. This didn't sit well with me because I like things to look neat and tidy, but it would have to suffice. I'm pretty good at making room for things, Mum always said that I could get two pounds of sugar into a pound bag! One of our neighbours also managed to find some room in her freezer to accommodate some of the food items.

We booked the DJ. I had prepared a list of songs that I knew Mum would like, and he confirmed that he would be happy to play them on the evening. He had a regular spot at a pub on the outskirts of town on a Friday evening and invited us to go along and have a chat to discuss our requirements in more detail. As it was a pub, we decided to have a couple of drinks while we were there - it would have been rude not to!

I had also booked a limousine, and Chris and I arranged to go and view it one evening to make sure that it was up to our expectations. We needn't have worried as the shiny white limousine was beautiful. The driver allowed me and Chris to sit inside, which was most enjoyable. The soft leather seating was very luxurious, and there was atmospheric lighting throughout the interior. We knew that Mum would love it.

We used to go over to Mum's most evenings, and suddenly we were going out and about, sorting all things party related. However, as this was in the run-up to Christmas, we could get away with saying that we were Christmas shopping. On the day before Mum's birthday, we made many trips to the venue, transporting food and all other necessary items. We had to come up with all kinds of excuses for Mum as it was unusual for me and Chris to be going out that often. Christmas had been and gone, so we were unable to continue using that as an excuse. We would tell Mum that we were going out to look for an accessory for our computer, because we knew that Mum wouldn't suggest coming with us as she didn't have an interest in computers. Or we would sometimes say that we were going out to look in one of our local DIY stores.

It was quite awkward getting items loaded into the car, with Mum living next door to us, and one of her windows looking directly out onto the car park where we were parked. It was also difficult when we spent time with Mum. We were constantly having to be careful as we didn't want to slip up and let the cat out of the bag regarding her party. However, all things party related were coming together, and Mum never suspected anything.

Finally, the long-awaited day arrived, and it was Mum's birthday. It was so exciting, and I knew that it was going to be an extra special birthday for her. Mum opened her presents in the morning. I had ordered some flowers for her, which were delivered mid-morning. It was a beautiful bouquet which contained roses, carnations, and chrysanthemums. As Mum loved flowers, she was delighted with them. After reading the card attached to the bouquet, she thanked me and gave me a hug with tears in her eyes. Friends called to see her with birthday gifts, and it was lovely to see Mum enjoying her special day.

Chris and I had lots to do in the afternoon. Mum knew she was going out for the evening, but she thought we were all going to a friend's house for food and drinks. Around lunchtime, Chris and I said that we would go and help the 'friend' prepare the food for the evening and anything else she needed help with, which was obviously a white lie. I hated lying to Mum but when you are planning a surprise party, unfortunately it does become necessary. I suggested that Mum relaxed and put her feet up in the afternoon while we were out, which she was happy to do.

So off we went to the venue where we would be joined by a little army of friends only too eager to help. A dear friend of ours came down from the north-east of England to help with the preparations at the venue, before attending the party and staying overnight. Everyone had turned up to help, so it was all hands on deck as we were all busy preparing food and decorating tables. We also collected a beautiful cake that had been made for Mum. It was a large, square, single-tiered fruit cake, which was decorated in white icing, with peach- coloured flowers piped around the edges. It looked beautiful.

I had found an old photograph of Mum when she was a baby and had made some 'then' and 'now' posters, which I was attaching to the venue walls along with banners and balloons. The DJ arrived to start setting up his music equipment, and I handed him the song list I had previously prepared. Everything was starting to come together and go as planned. Each plate of food was covered and placed in the refrigerators in the kitchen of the venue. A friend had kindly offered to go back to the venue roughly an hour before guests started arriving to lay out all the food, still covered of course. It was to be placed on a long table with the birthday cake taking pride of place in the centre, along with a photograph of Mum to the side of it. I appreciated her taking the time to set out the food as it meant that Chris and I could get everything organised at home and help Mum get ready for the evening. Mum was really looking forward to what she thought was, 'going to a friend's for the evening.' I thought to myself, *Is she in for a surprise!*

The guests were due to turn up at the venue by

7 pm as we would be arriving with Mum at 7:30 pm. I wanted everyone to be settled with their drinks when Mum walked in. We told Mum that we had booked a taxi for 6:30 pm. At 6:15 pm, I suggested that we made our way outside and waited for the taxi to arrive. Little did Mum know that she would be travelling to the venue in a white limousine. We had booked the limo to pick us up at 6:30 pm and wanted to make sure that Mum was outside when it pulled up. She would be chauffeured around our local town for an hour before we were dropped off at the party venue.

We stood outside eagerly waiting, and at exactly 6:30 pm we observed the beautiful white limousine entering the Close. I had prearranged with the driver for him to get out of the car and ask for Mum, which he was more than happy to oblige. The limo pulled up at the front of our building, and the chauffeur got out. Mum said, 'I bet he's lost.' The way the properties are numbered is quite unusual where we live, and everyone appears to get lost.

He started walking towards us and as he moved closer, he said, 'Have we got the birthday girl here?'

'That's me,' replied Mum.

He then said, 'Happy Birthday, we've got a limo for you, darling.'

I will never forget the look on Mum's face as she was escorted up to the waiting limousine, it was priceless.

We settled into the plush leather seats and the chauffer poured a glass of champagne for each of us before we glided off. There were five of us in the limousine which meant that it was nice and comfortable. I had invited two of our neighbours to join us for the journey, and they had been outside with us waiting for the car to arrive. I had put together a music CD of some of Mum's favourite old songs, which we listened to on the journey. Funnily enough, Mum still thought that she was going to a friend's house for drinks and food, as we kept up the pretence. We were chauffeured around, listening to music, drinking champagne, and feeling very special.

We arrived at the venue at 7:30 pm, and I thought that as soon as we pulled up outside, Mum was going to suspect that something was going on. She had been to other functions there in the past, so she would definitely recognise the place - or so we thought! However, the venue wasn't that well-lit, and Mum's eyesight wasn't at its best, so she didn't recognise the place. She did, however, wonder why we had pulled up there when we were supposed to be going to a friend's house. The driver said that his fuel light kept coming on, and that he needed to get some more petrol. So, we all got out of the limousine, and the driver promised that he would come back for us once he had filled up at the garage just up the road from the venue. He informed us that he wasn't allowed to fill the car with fuel when he had passengers on board. This story had been prearranged with the driver to throw Mum off the scent, and she believed it.

We now needed to get Mum inside. We knew the driver wasn't coming back for us as our one-hour journey had finished. I told Mum that I was going inside the building to use the ladies, and everyone piped up saying that we might as well all go while we were there.

As we entered the building, I felt sure that Mum would recognise where we were, but surprisingly she didn't; she even asked where the ladies were. I directed her towards a door which she opened to be met by friends and neighbours who were cheering, and the song 'Happy Birthday' by Stevie Wonder started playing. The look on Mum's face was priceless, she was overwhelmed, and I was so relieved that everything had gone to plan.

There were friends there that Mum hadn't seen for many years, and there were also friends of mine that I hadn't seen for a long time, so it was lovely to be spending the evening with them. I would have liked to invite Lisa, but I no longer had any contact details for her. I had invited John's mum, and it was good to see her. She told me that John had spent some time living and working in Germany. Mum enjoyed catching up with her and other old friends. She received some beautiful birthday cards and gifts, and thoroughly enjoyed the evening. It had been a good night; everything had gone to plan, and Mum stated it was one of the best nights of her life. She would treasure the memories always!

Unfortunately, Chris wasn't feeling too well on the evening of the party as she had been experiencing a few breathing problems on the days prior to the event, so I was quite concerned about her. She was planning on visiting her GP the following week, but then her symptoms appeared to subside.

I thought that 2009 had started off well. We had all enjoyed the Christmas and New Year festivities, and of course Mum's seventieth birthday celebrations.

A few weeks after Mum's party, Chris started to struggle with her breathing again. Worried about her,

I called an ambulance in the early hours of the morning. She was rushed into hospital, where she remained for ten days. She was unwell and was diagnosed with pulmonary oedema. The doctors had stated that the condition had been caused by heart failure. This was a huge concern for all of us. Her angina had returned several years earlier, and if that wasn't bad enough, she was now faced with something else which was heart related. Unfortunately, the problems Chris had with her breathing seemed to be ongoing and she was admitted to hospital again in April with the same problem. This year was not going well at all, as Chris seemed to be in and out of hospital due to having fluid on her lungs.

Then, in July, Mum suffered a heart attack and was rushed into hospital. I asked the hospital receptionist when I could go in to see Mum. I gave her Mum's name and details and informed her that Mum would be frightened and upset, and she would want me to be with her. At that point, the receptionist said, 'Well it's not up to your mum, it's up to the nurse in charge. Sit down, I'll let you know when you can go in.' I did as I was instructed. I went and sat down with Chris and just burst into tears. I was appalled at the attitude of the receptionist. I thought to myself, *She certainly skipped charm school.* Luckily, it wasn't too much longer before I was allowed to go in to see Mum.

She was comfortable, and later admitted to the Coronary Care Unit. It was a quiet ward, and the nurses were very attentive. Mum was looked after extremely well. The main visiting time was during the afternoon and evening, although they did allow one visitor for a morning visit. Mum told me not to bother trailing up to visit in the morning as it was only for a short period. I kissed her goodbye and said that I would see her the next day. She reminded me not to bother going for the half-hour visit the following morning. I said, 'Okay.' I had every intention of going!

The following morning came, and I set off for the hospital. The ward doors opened, and I walked in. Mum was sitting in a chair at the side of her bed, and as soon as she saw me, her face lit up. I walked over to her, gave her a hug and a kiss, and with tears in her eyes she whispered, 'I'm so glad you've come.' I will never forget how pleased she looked to see me. There had never been any doubt that I would go and see her that morning. She remained on the Coronary Care Unit for a few days and was then transferred to one of the other wards for a few more days before being discharged.

If Mum being in hospital wasn't bad enough, someone smashed into our car in the hospital car park one day when we were visiting her. There was a lot of damage done to the car, but luckily the driver had left his details under the windscreen wipers. Apart from Mum's seventieth birthday party, this had not been a good year, all things considered.

To try and raise our spirits, I booked tickets for the three of us to see The Nolans in concert on 1st November at Sheffield City Hall. This group of sisters were very popular in the 1970s and 1980s, and we all enjoyed listening to their music. This would give us something to look forward to, and I was just hoping and praying that Mum and Chris would be well enough to go on the night. The evening arrived, and thankfully they were okay, and excited about the concert. I had booked front row seats, and it was a brilliant evening from start to finish. We were clapping and singing along to the songs that we had always enjoyed listening to. I was so pleased that I had decided to do this for Mum and Chris as it had brought some light relief during a challenging year.

CHAPTER 27

My Fiftieth Birthday

I t was 2011, and my fiftieth birthday was fast approaching. I wasn't too happy when I reached forty, and now, in what seemed like no time at all, I was about to become fifty. I knew that Mum and Chris wanted to do something special for my birthday. They both asked if I would like a party, but I wasn't that bothered. A party takes a lot of planning, and neither Mum nor Chris was fit enough to organise a party. They suggested that weather permitting, we could go to the coast for the day and have a nice meal while we were there. In the evening, we would go to Mum's for a drink and some food. This was a great idea; I was happy with their suggestion and was looking forward to my birthday.

A few days before my birthday, we went to a Jane McDonald concert in York, which was part of my birthday present from Mum and Chris. It was debateable whether we would get to the concert as Chris had an infection in her foot and was unable to put her shoe on. However, Chris was determined that we were going to York, so she drove with a slipper on the affected foot. It wasn't ideal, but she was a good driver, and she managed quite well.

The following day, the infection in Chris's foot had become more severe, to the point where she had to attend the emergency department at our local hospital. She was diagnosed with cellulitis and was informed by the medical team that she would need to be admitted as she required intravenous antibiotics. This didn't come as a surprise because Chris had been admitted to hospital in the past with the same problem. However, on this occasion the infection was more severe.

So now it was just a matter of waiting until a bed became available for her. We were waiting at the hospital for what seemed like hours. Suddenly, Chris was informed that there were no beds available there, or at any of the other hospitals where patients are often transferred if there is no availability at our local hospital. I found it hard to believe that out of four possible hospitals, there wasn't a bed available at any of them, but apparently that was the situation.

They suggested that Chris received the antibiotic injections at home. Chris and I were not happy about this. It wasn't an ideal situation, but she needed the antibiotics, so she went along with their suggestion. Consequently, Chris was sent home late in the evening with a cannula in the back of her hand and informed that the Community Intervention Team (C.I.T) nurses would call to administer intravenous antibiotics at home.

The next day, the nursing team made an initial visit to explain what the procedure would be, and how often they would be calling. They informed Chris that they would need to call four times a day to administer the medication. They stated that they would call at 6 am, midday, 6 pm and midnight. This wasn't ideal, but it was imperative that Chris received the necessary medication, and in order to do this, Chris had to be available at those times.

We were getting up at 5 am, ready for the nurses coming at 6 am. The following two visits during the day weren't too bad. Then there was the midnight visit, which very often ended up being 12:30 am before they arrived. The antibiotic solution had to be freshly mixed in our home on each visit, which took time. The nurses also had to complete paperwork. Therefore, they would often not leave until after 1 am. This meant that Chris and I weren't getting to bed until around 1:30 am and we had to be back up again at 5 am, ready for another nurse calling at 6 am. Chris stated on several occasions that I didn't need to get up at the same time as her in the morning or stay up until midnight each evening. However, I wanted to be there for Chris when the nurses arrived. If I had stayed in bed, my sleep would have been disturbed when they arrived, so it was just as easy for me to get up with Chris.

Chris asked the nurse if she would be able to mix up a batch of the antibiotic ready for the following visit. We thought this would save time. However, the nurse informed us that this would not be possible. She explained that the solution had to be made up fresh prior to each injection. We appreciated what she was telling us. It was just a thought.

This was turning into a nightmare as we were hardly getting any sleep. We were shattered. If that wasn't bad enough, every few days Chris had to attend the hospital to have her cannula taken out and a fresh one inserted, because they are only supposed to be in place for so many days before they need changing. This was starting to resemble something akin to a comedy film. Chris did say that if ever she got an infection like this again, where she needed intravenous antibiotics, she would flatly refuse to be treated at home. She stated that she would wait at the hospital until they found her a bed somewhere, as it had not been easy having the treatment at home. On the plus side, the antibiotics were obviously doing their job because Chris's foot started to improve.

In the middle of all this, it was my birthday. In these circumstances, there was no way we would be going to the coast, and it was debateable whether we would still be able to go for the meal that we had planned. It didn't matter to me; I was more concerned about Chris's foot than anything else. Although the nurses were still visiting, there had been a significant improvement in Chris's foot which meant that she was now able to put shoes on and drive comfortably. Once the lunchtime nurse had been, we got in the car and headed off for my birthday meal. We knew we had to be back home for the nurse calling at teatime, but at least we had a few hours free to enjoy a meal and unwind.

In the evening, as planned, we went to Mum's for a drink. They had a beautiful cake made for me, which was piped with pink and white icing, and a ribbon surrounded the sides. When they lit the candles and sang happy birthday, I felt so special. I received some lovely cards and gifts. Mum and Chris bought me a beautiful watch between them, along with some other presents, which I will always treasure. Due to the situation with Chris's foot, it hadn't quite been the birthday that Chris and Mum had planned for me. However, I had enjoyed my fiftieth birthday and appreciated everything Mum and Chris had done to make it as special as possible.

The infection in Chris's foot went on to get better. Consequently, the antibiotic injections ceased, and the nurses no longer had to visit. We were relieved. At last, we could catch up on some sleep.

CHAPTER 28

My Greatest Loss

In 2012, Mum was having quite a few health problems. Three years after her heart attack, she had started to suffer with fluid on her lungs, which meant that there were periods when she was experiencing quite severe breathing problems. This resulted in her having to stay overnight in hospital on a couple of occasions. It seemed that her health was going downhill, and Chris's health problems were ever-present. They were both quite unwell, and I was worried sick about them.

If Mum and Chris's health problems weren't enough to contend with, I was diagnosed with a tumour. Nausea rose from the pit of my stomach when the consultant delivered the news. I looked at Chris's ashen face. She reached for my hand and squeezed it. Luckily, the tumour was benign, but it needed to be removed. In February 2013, I was admitted to hospital for the removal of a salivary gland tumour. I spent a day and a half in hospital and was then discharged. Recovery went well. Apart from having a row of stitches at the side of my neck, I felt okay. This wasn't a good start to the year, and at this point we assumed that things could only get better.

In July 2013, we went on holiday to the North Yorkshire coastal resort of Scarborough for two weeks and the weather was glorious. Mum wasn't in the best of health while we were there, although we were having a heatwave and the hot weather always affected her. She had been unwell on and off for most of the year and had been taken to hospital several times by ambulance. A few days after we returned from holiday, Mum took ill again and was admitted to hospital where she stayed for a couple of days. She was up and down with her health and was just trying to make the best of the situation. She was never the type to give in. If she felt that she could keep going, she would do.

In August 2013, Mum's health seemed to deteriorate further, to the point where she was having bouts of breathing difficulties more frequently. One evening, Chris and I were at Mum's having a drink and a chat, and she seemed in good spirits. She was brighter, and more like her old self. We talked about anything and everything which was usual for us, and we always ended up having a good laugh about something. We had watched a bit of TV and ate some supper, and Mum said that she felt better that evening than she had done for a long time. She felt as though she had turned a corner and was on the mend. I was so pleased, and I went to bed that night with my spirits uplifted. I felt happy and was so relieved that Mum was feeling better.

The following morning, as usual, Chris and I went over to Mum's to have an early morning cuppa with her. We had a key, so we let ourselves in. I found it strange that Mum was still in bed, as she would normally have been up at that time. I wondered if she had had a bad night and was staying in bed a while longer. I gave it a few minutes, then went into the bedroom to wake her up because time was getting on, and I knew she would want to be up. I shouted her several times but was getting no response. I went back to Chris and told her that I couldn't wake Mum up.

She came into the bedroom and advised me to get our neighbour, Angie, who was a nurse. I rushed straight over to Angie's and started banging on her door and shouting for her. She opened the door; while sobbing, I told her that we couldn't wake Mum up. She came immediately and confirmed that Mum had passed away. I was numb. I was in a terrible state. I felt as though my whole world had ended. She had told me the previous evening that she felt so much better, so why had this happened? She was my rock, my mentor, and my best friend. I was an only child and not only were we mother and daughter, but we were also best friends. She was the kindest, friendliest, and most gentle person that I ever knew, and I was so proud to have her as my mum. I worshipped the ground she walked on. I was absolutely devastated and could not begin to imagine how I would be able to carry on without her.

I was unable to do anything as I was in such a state. I couldn't function. Nothing made sense anymore. I was just walking around in a daze. Thankfully, Angie informed the relevant people, and she stayed with Chris and I for most of the day. She was brilliant, and I don't know what we would have done without her that day.

I went to bed that evening but didn't sleep at all

because there were endless questions swirling around in my head. At 5 am the following morning, I woke Chris up as I felt that things needed sorting at Mum's.

'We need to contact the funeral directors,' I said, sitting bolt upright in bed.

'Sweetheart, it's 5 am on a Sunday morning! We can't organise anything today.'

'There are things we need to do,' I insisted.

'Okay, I'm getting up,' was her reply.

We both went across to Mum's, made a drink, and just sat there. Chris was right, there was nothing we could have organised at that time on a Sunday morning. I then felt guilty for getting her out of bed at 5 am and insisted that she went back to bed, while I remained at Mum's as I was unable to sleep.

I had to do all the things that one has to do when someone passes away and it was the first time that I had ever had to do this. I was finding it so difficult, trying to deal with everything that needed doing. There was a funeral to organise, and I could not imagine how I would cope with the arrangements. Also, at some point, we would have to start emptying Mum's home as she was in rented accommodation. Chris was always by my side and assured me that we would get through it together.

It was later confirmed that Mum had passed away due to heart-related problems.

We booked an appointment with the funeral directors to make the arrangements. We had an appointment with a lady by the name of Julie, and she was lovely. She offered her condolences and made us feel as much at ease as she could under the circumstances. We started talking about Mum, and within minutes I was in floods of tears. I can recall Julie crouching down at the side of me and handing me tissues. She made Chris and I a drink, and we talked in general about Mum.

However, we had gone there to make the funeral arrangements, so I thought we needed to begin, although Julie wasn't rushing us in any way. I didn't know where to start because I had never had to do anything like this in the past. I couldn't think straight and was finding the entire process too emotional. We eventually managed to make a start with the arrangements, and Julie was so compassionate. I was unable to sort everything out during one visit as I found it too upsetting, so we made further appointments.

Thankfully, I knew what Mum's wishes were for her funeral. However, it was only during the past year that this had been discussed. That was partly down to me as I never felt comfortable talking about funeral arrangements. She would bring up the subject, but I would never discuss it as I didn't want to think of a time when I wouldn't have Mum. I gave it some thought and realised that it did need talking about because I would need to know exactly what Mum's requests were for her funeral. I had a pretty good idea, but we needed to discuss it properly. I was so pleased that the conversation had taken place as I was aware of her exact requirements now that she had passed away.

The day of the funeral arrived, and I was numb. I was a complete mess and could not begin to imagine how I would get through the day. I was unable to focus on anything, and I knew that this was going to be the most difficult day of my life. I was so pleased that I had Chris by my side as there was no way I could have got through the day without her.

Following the funeral, things went from bad to worse. I couldn't sleep, I wasn't eating properly, and just trying to function on a daily basis was becoming increasingly difficult. I missed Mum so much and felt that my heart had been broken in two. I just seemed to withdraw from everything. I had endless support from Chris, who had been a close friend of Mum's for over thirty years, so as you can imagine she was devastated too.

I was in a dark place, and consequently, my panic attacks became more frequent, and I was forced to seek help from my GP. I was prescribed a week's course of diazepam, which was a drug that would hopefully relax me and help me to sleep. This was not the road I wanted to go down as I did not want to feel as though I was becoming dependent on what seemed to be the easy answer. I decided not to take the tablets because I felt that this was the correct decision for me at the time.

'You've done exactly what your mum told me you would do when she passed away,' Chris said.

'What's that?'

'You've gone to pieces,' she replied.

Nothing seemed to make sense anymore. Mum and I were so close, we always had each other, and we didn't let a day pass when we didn't hug and say that we loved each other. We went everywhere together, so consequently I found myself avoiding places that we had previously visited. It was easier to do that than explain where Mum was whenever people asked. I found that I was avoiding going out more and more. It felt as though a part of me was missing, and of course it was - Mum!

Christmas was undoubtedly the worst time of the year for me. How were we ever going to get through Christmas without Mum? As everyone knows, Christmas starts in August, which is when the majority of the shops start to display their festive products. I hated seeing all the cards and gifts in the shops and felt that I wanted to steer clear of all things Christmas related. Mum loved this time of year. Making lists and choosing gifts was something that she enjoyed immensely.

She loved to have her home decorated and would often sit for long periods watching the lights as they flickered and sparkled on the Christmas tree. On Christmas morning, she was filled with excitement when we all opened our presents together, while festive songs were playing in the background. I loved spoiling Mum and always made sure that she had lots of lovely gifts to open.

While the Christmas dinner was cooking, we would partake in a sherry - or two - and raise a glass to absent friends. Mum made the best Christmas dinner - along with all the other mums of course. Everything was cooked to perfection, and there was plenty of it. No one ever left the table feeling hungry. We always had such a lovely day, and as I looked back, I could never have imagined that 2012 would be our last Christmas together.

The funeral home had a memorial tree in their reception area, and Chris and I were invited to place a memorial tag on the tree in memory of Mum. We went along and the tree looked beautiful, as the white lights sparkled. We asked if Julie was available, and she came out, gave us both a hug, and asked how we were doing. We then wrote on the memorial tags and looked for a suitable position on the tree to hang them. There were quite a lot of tags on the tree, placed there by other people in memory of their loved ones.

I continued to look around the tree, and Julie said something to me which I have never forgotten. She said, 'What about up here, at the top, where Mum belongs?' I thought it was a lovely thing to say. Those words meant so much to me and will stay with me always. I don't know whether Julie noticed, but I was struggling to hold back the tears as we left. Each year, Chris and I would take a gift in for Julie and her colleagues to share in the office.

Chris and I could not imagine how we were going to get through Christmas 2013. It would be our first Christmas without Mum. We wanted to keep it low-key, in the way that we didn't put up any decorations. We wanted our home to look as normal as possible, that way we could almost pretend that Christmas wasn't happening. This was a terrible time for us, but we did get through it because we remained strong for each other.

CHAPTER 29

A Much-Needed Holiday

I t was 2014, and Chris and I felt that we needed a holiday. We normally went to Scarborough with Mum so we were unsure whether we wanted to return as it would bring back too many memories. However, we were used to the place that we usually stayed in, it was close to all amenities and suited our needs, so we decided to book. We stayed at the Friarage apartments in the centre of Scarborough, which are four-star self-catering properties owned and run by the lovely Steff and her husband. It is about a ten minute-walk to the beach, but unfortunately, we didn't have a sea view from our property. The apartment we stayed in was on the ground floor, which was ideal for us as we both had mobility issues.

The day of our holiday arrived, and although we didn't have the level of excitement we would normally have had, we were still looking forward to a break, and some much- needed sea air. We arrived at the property, unloaded the car, and took our luggage inside. As soon as I walked into the apartment, I became emotional as I was thinking back to the previous year when Mum was with us. Chris and I did all the usual things we would normally have done when Mum was with us, though we never used to go mad, as none of us were fit enough. We went to our favourite fish and chip restaurant where we had been with Mum. It was lovely, as it overlooked the sea. Later, we would walk along the sea front while enjoying an ice cream and looking at the boats in the harbour. Although it was a difficult holiday, due to the absence of Mum, it was lovely to be away from home as it had been a tough year, and we just felt as though we needed a break.

We stayed in Scarborough for ten days and returned home feeling refreshed. However, three days after we had returned home, Chris seemed confused and wasn't responding well when I was talking to her. I knew immediately that something was wrong. I suspected that she had suffered a stroke, all the signs were there. I phoned Angie, our neighbour, who was a nurse. She came straight away and confirmed that Chris had suffered a stroke, so we rang for an ambulance immediately. I was devastated and shocked. She was taken to our local hospital, where she was admitted onto the stroke unit. Things weren't good, she was unable to speak properly, and she had lost all feeling down one side of her body. She was unable to feed herself and needed the assistance of the nurses, or I would feed her. It was heart-breaking to see.

Days went on, and there seemed to be little improvement in Chris's condition. A speech therapist and physiotherapist visited her daily at her bedside. Finally, Chris's speech, along with movement of limbs, started to improve. One day at visiting time, I walked onto the ward and as I turned the corner, I could see that Chris was sitting in the chair at the side of her bed. As I walked down the corridor, she spotted me, raised her arm, and waved. This was the arm that she had previously been unable to move. I walked into the bay with tears streaming down my face and gave her the biggest hug. I was elated. The physiotherapy was obviously working, and this was a step in the right direction for Chris.

We talked, and she revealed that she was starting to feel better and was now able to do more things for herself. She looked at me and said, 'How are you coping?'

'Don't worry about me, I'm fine,' I assured her.

'I'm wondering how much more you can take.'

'Just concentrate on getting better. I'm doing okay,' I replied.

Obviously, I wasn't okay, but I wasn't going to share that information with her. I was worried sick about Chris and what the long-term effects of her stroke would be. She needed to concentrate on getting herself better, without the added stress of worrying about me.

The vascular surgeon had been to see Chris and informed her that her carotid arteries were severely blocked. This is what had caused her to have a stroke. He informed us that ideally, the arteries needed unblocking, which would mean Chris going into theatre and having a general anaesthetic so that the procedure could be performed. He was reluctant to do the operation as Chris more than likely wouldn't survive the anaesthetic because of the condition of her heart. He stated that it would be extremely unlikely that an anaesthetist would agree to administer a general anaesthetic due to Chris's state of health. So, it was agreed that Chris would be put on a new blood-thinning drug, which would hopefully keep the blood flowing correctly through the carotid arteries. This new medication was superior to the previous blood-thinning medication that Chris had been taking. Chris's condition continued to improve, and she was discharged from hospital.

The new medication was causing some problems for Chris. Two days after leaving hospital, she started to experience severe nose bleeds. She was losing a lot of blood and was advised to attend the emergency department at our local hospital. They examined Chris and decided to cauterize the inside of her nose to stop the bleeding. The new medication was very good, in the way that it was allowing the flow of blood to run freely through her arteries, but it was also causing the nose bleeds.

As well as the nose bleeds, Chris started to bruise easily. She only had to brush past something firmly with her arms and she would bruise. While she was on this medication, I can't remember a time when she didn't have bruises on her arms. Also, she had to be so careful not to cut herself. There were a couple of occasions when she did encounter a small cut on her hand or finger, and it would take a long time for the bleeding to stop. These were some of the side-effects of this new medication, but primarily, it was doing its job in keeping the blood thin and flowing through the arteries. This would hopefully prevent Chris from having another stroke.

Chris had to inform the Driver and Vehicle Licensing Agency of her stroke, and they advised her to refrain from driving for one month. If, within that month, she didn't suffer a further stroke, she would be allowed to resume driving. Chris's ongoing health problems meant that she was unable to walk far and needed the use of the car. However, she had been instructed not to drive so that was the situation. I have never known a month seem so long. Fortunately, Chris didn't have another stroke, so she was able to get back behind the wheel, when permitted.

She seemed to recover from the stroke pretty well, although she did struggle at times with speech, but that appeared to be sporadic. I couldn't believe what had happened, and what a terrible time we were having. Less than a year after Mum had passed away, we were faced with this. Chris was still independent and was able to get around and do everything for herself, but things had changed. She found it difficult to remember certain things, and at times, she would appear vague if we were having a conversation. I was still struggling following the loss of Mum, and the following year I lost a big part of Chris. She was never the same.

CHAPTER 30

Counselling

I realised that I could not continue indefinitely the way I was. I had endless support from Chris, but she wasn't a trained counsellor, plus she was dealing with her own grief and recovering from a stroke. I went back to see my GP, and it was suggested that I have counselling. At first, I wasn't too keen on the idea because I have always been the type of person who likes to keep things private and have never felt comfortable with the idea of opening up to people. Also, it would appear that people can no longer just be depressed or have anxiety problems as it has a stigma attached to it nowadays. It would appear that these people now fall into the category of being described as having 'mental health issues' which is not a description that I favour.

However, I was getting desperate and knew that something needed to be done. There was a waiting list for the service - as you would expect, but eventually I was offered an appointment with a therapist. I attended the appointment feeling optimistic. I chatted to the therapist and was given a lot of useful information.

We talked about my phobias and how they made me feel. The therapist explained the term 'fight or flight' stating that when someone is experiencing a panic attack their heart starts racing, and they start to sweat and feel sick.

An anxiety disorder results when the 'fight or flight' response becomes triggered too easily and too frequently. These were all the symptoms I was experiencing so I could relate to what was being said. I was told that if I found myself in a situation where I needed to use 'fight or flight,' the anxiety at that moment would only reach a certain level, and then it would start to reduce back down to an acceptable level. The therapist said that inhaling and then exhaling slowly would help. She stated that no one had ever died from having an anxiety attack, which was reassuring!

I was also told that the only way to overcome my fears would be to tackle them head on. The therapist suggested that I force myself to go in a lift, and on a train. I could see her reasoning behind this, but it was never going to happen. You wouldn't throw someone into a river if they couldn't swim.

I saw this therapist several times, and then I was allocated a different counsellor covering the same issues. Soon after, I was assigned yet another therapist. It seemed that as soon as I was starting to make progress and feel comfortable with one person, I was being passed on to a different therapist. The counselling was not going well, and I didn't feel that I was benefitting from the service at that time. It was then established that I needed bereavement counselling, so I went to see another counsellor. It was starting to become frustrating because each time I was introduced to a new counsellor, I had to go right back to the beginning and start explaining everything, which was causing me further stress.

At my first appointment with my new counsellor, who would be concentrating solely on bereavement therapy, I asked her if she had suffered a bereavement herself. She said that she had lost someone she was close to. That said, I felt that she was able to offer me counselling. Now some people may find this a little strange, but I feel that in order to fully understand how a bereaved person is feeling and be able to offer counselling, you need to have experienced a bereavement yourself. I appreciate that counsellors will have extensive training in their chosen field, and I am in no way disrespecting them as they provide a good service. However, I would not feel happy accepting bereavement counselling from someone who has never been bereaved. How could they possibly understand the heartache a person is feeling? That is not something that can be taught, it must be felt.

So, it was back to the beginning again as I started to explain the loss of Mum and how my world had been shattered. The counsellor was sympathetic and talked about the loss she had suffered. At one point I thought, *Who's counselling who here?* The appointments with her were normally for one hour and during that hour we would talk about lots of things. We didn't always just discuss bereavement, although that was the main topic. We also talked about holidays and just general day-to-day stuff. I felt as though I was connecting with her and that she was going to be good for me.

She put me at ease, and I felt more relaxed with her than I had with any of the other counsellors. She had a calming voice, and I just knew that we were going to work well together. I felt that I had at last found the perfect counsellor. I disclosed that I was having problems sleeping and that it was very rare that I slept for more than three or four hours a night. We talked about this, and I told her that as soon as I went to bed a thousand memories about Mum came flooding into my mind. She then suggested that we tried Eye Movement Desensitisation and Reprocessing (EMDR) therapy. This is a therapy that enables people to heal from the symptoms and emotional distress that are the result of disturbing life experiences. So, this was what we were working towards. However, we never got around to starting the EMDR therapy.

After each appointment, I felt as though I was getting a little bit further forward. Talking to her was therapeutic. I told her that I wrote poetry, and she asked me to take some poems in for her to read, which I did, and she thought they were very good. The sessions continued until October 2017 when I had to go into hospital for planned surgery on my knee. My mobility would be restricted post-surgery therefore I would not be able to attend any sessions for a few weeks. My operation came and went, and I was able to recommence counselling in January 2018. However, I found out that this was to be my last appointment with the counsellor as she informed me that she was leaving due to family commitments - I was gutted!

She was the only one who had made a difference since I had started with the counselling service. I felt as though we were getting somewhere, and I was looking forward to brighter days ahead. I feel that if I had been able to continue with her, my future would have been somewhat different. The one person who was making me see things more clearly was exiting my life. Nevertheless, I wished her well in her new adventure.

For me, that was to be the end of bereavement counselling as I did not feel that I could cope with seeing someone new and having to start explaining my story right from the beginning, yet again.

CHAPTER 31

Chris's Seventieth Birthday

Chris's seventieth birthday was fast approaching, and as you will imagine, I wanted to do something special. As my present to her, I booked a four-day break in York. We stayed in a modern, self-catering apartment right in the centre of this historic city, which was established by the Romans. Part of the stone city walls, built by the Romans, still stand, as well as many medieval, timber-framed buildings. We were relatively close to everywhere we were likely to go. I would cook breakfast every morning, which would set us up for most of the day, then anything else we wanted to eat was purchased while we were out. This is what we have always preferred to do, no matter where we have gone. We would go out for the day, browsing in the shops on the narrow, medieval streets, making our way to the majestic York Minster.

As this was a special birthday for Chris, I wanted the holiday to be extra special. With all the health problems that Chris had, I knew that the chance of her reaching another milestone birthday would be slim. In fact, to be honest, her health was so poor that I was both surprised and relieved that she had reached seventy.

I bought banners, balloons and all things birthday related to decorate the apartment on the day of her birthday. I had also ordered a birthday cake, which I collected while we were in York and managed to hide in the apartment until the morning of her birthday. She was special, and I wanted to make this a day that she would always remember. We had a lovely time, the apartment was beautiful, the weather stayed fine, and despite Chris's health problems, she had thoroughly enjoyed herself.

We returned home, and I knew that I would be going into hospital later in the year for a total knee replacement, so I was trying to get myself into the right mindset for that. This was to be major knee surgery, which would leave me incapacitated for several weeks. Chris's health was up and down. She had been in hospital a couple of times overnight due to slight infections, but everything seemed stable with her.

The day for me to go into hospital for surgery arrived, and although I was reluctant to leave Chris at home on her own, it was surgery that I needed to have. Fortunately, one of our neighbours said that she would keep an eye on Chris while I was in hospital. This was a relief. Although I was still concerned, I did feel happier about going into hospital knowing that Chris would have some support at home. My surgery took place, and I was in hospital for four days, then discharged, with a walking frame and crutches.

Despite Chris's own health problems, she was prepared to look after me, to the best of her ability, now that I had returned home from hospital. I was observing Chris, and she didn't seem to be her usual self. She appeared to be somewhat confused. I was concerned, but she assured me that she was okay. However, the following day Chris was taken into hospital. The doctors diagnosed several infections throughout her body. I was discharged from hospital on the Monday, and Chris was admitted to hospital on the Tuesday. You couldn't make it up. This was a nightmare. This could only happen to us. I was so upset that I wouldn't be able to visit Chris while she was in hospital as I could hardly walk. I don't use lifts, and there was no way I would have been able to manage all the stairs up to the ward.

Our neighbour helped me to pack a bag, which she later took up to the hospital for Chris once she was settled on a ward. I had just had major knee surgery and I was now home alone. Luckily, I had done quite a lot of batch cooking before I went into hospital, so there were plenty of ready meals available that just needed heating through. I was so pleased that I had decided to prepare the meals before my operation, because there was no way I could have stood for long enough to cook a meal from scratch. Also, as Christmas was only a few weeks away, Chris and I had done the majority of our shopping since I knew I would struggle to get out and about following my knee surgery.

One of our neighbours popped in occasionally to check if I was okay, and if I needed anything, and a couple of friends also offered to help. I was okay for food; the only items I ran out of were bread and milk, which my neighbour brought for me. Initially, I was having to stand up in the kitchen to eat my meals because I was unable to carry a plate of food to the dining table as I was using a walking frame. My neighbour brought me a stool over from her house, so I was now able to sit down in the kitchen to eat my meals, which was much better.

I wasn't allowed to take a shower at this stage post-surgery, so I had to make do with a stripped wash. It wasn't ideal, but it was the only way of keeping myself clean. I was used to showering either once or twice a day, so this way of keeping clean didn't sit well with me. However, it would have to suffice. I was struggling, as my knee wasn't flexible, and I was scared to let go of my crutches. My neighbour offered to help me to have a wash. I was grateful for her offer, but there are only so many things that you allow the neighbours to help with. I declined her offer. I would manage.

I was missing Chris so much and just wanted her back home with me. For the first time ever, I was unable to visit her in hospital, and it was upsetting me immensely. However, circumstances wouldn't allow me to visit on this occasion. It was the same for Chris in hospital - she was missing me and wanted to be back home. There were lots of long phone calls, texts, and plenty of tears between us, on a daily basis.

Finally, the day arrived for Chris to be discharged. She had been in hospital for eight days, and we had both found our enforced separation extremely difficult. I noticed that she had lost some weight, but other than that, she looked quite well. It was lovely to have her back home, where she belonged. It was now a matter of trying to look after each other the best way we could.

Christmas came around, and it proved to be quite a testing time. Chris started to feel unwell again, though she didn't need to be hospitalised on this occasion. I was still hobbling around on crutches, which meant that we were unable to get out to do everything we would normally have done in preparation for Christmas. As far as I was concerned, it didn't matter. We were together, and we were happy. We would make the following Christmas extra special. It would be better - or so I thought!

CHAPTER 32

Our Final Goodbye

I t was 2018, and Chris's health seemed to be okay at the beginning of the year. We normally started planning our summer holiday at this time of the year, so we were able to get booked in on the dates that we chose. However, this year, we both decided that rather than going on holiday for one or two weeks, we would just stick to having days out. This arrangement suited us both, and we were looking forward to the summer.

Months went on and Chris's health problems were ever-present. She was up and down with numerous issues, and she couldn't seem to get any further forward healthwise. She constantly felt tired and had little energy. In May, Chris had an appointment with one of the nurses at her GP's surgery. While we were in the surgery, Chris became more unwell, so the nurse asked the GP to examine Chris. He did several tests on her and took some blood. She wasn't too well at all; the doctor wasn't happy, and he advised that she went to hospital by ambulance.

When we arrived at the hospital, Chris was taken to a bed almost straight away. Along with all her other health issues, she had now been informed that there was a problem with her potassium levels. The doctor stated that he wanted to revise her medication and that Chris would probably be in hospital for two or three days. She was very tired, and just wanted to sleep, so I left the hospital around 9 pm and went home to pack a bag for her, ready to take with me the following day.

However, in the early hours of the morning, I was woken up by a phone call from the hospital, saying that Chris's condition had deteriorated, and it would be advisable for me to go to the hospital right away. I phoned my neighbour, and in less than half an hour we were up at the hospital. I arrived on the ward and went straight to the bed where Chris had been when I had left her the previous evening. It was empty. A nurse informed me that Chris had suffered a heart attack and passed away. I was absolutely devastated. I felt that my whole world had ended right there and then. I could never have imagined that when I walked off the ward the previous evening, it would be the last time I saw Chris alive.

We had lived together for thirty-two years and shared everything. How was I going to carry on? Why had this happened to me again? I had nothing left. I was struggling to make sense of everything. I still hadn't come to terms with losing Mum, and now I was faced with another loss. Chris had been my rock since losing Mum, she was the one person who had been keeping me going. She was the glue that was holding me together. Suddenly she was no longer here, and I couldn't see a way forward. For me, that was it. I felt that I had nothing left to live for. Everything had been taken away from me.

For the first time in my life, I was living on my own. My home felt cold and empty, the silence was deafening. I barely ate anything the week following Chris's death as her passing had had a major effect on my health. I was walking around in a daze, and just generally unable to function. There would be another funeral to organise, and I didn't feel that I would be capable of making the arrangements. However, it had to be done.

The funeral was organised by the same funeral directors that I had used for Mum's funeral. They were very good, and I specified that I would like Julie to take care of the arrangements as she had been so compassionate following the death of Mum. She could see that I was in such a state, and she did an excellent job in taking as much pressure off me as she could. She even attended Chris's funeral, in order to support me. I thought this was so caring and felt that it was above and beyond the call of duty. We have kept in touch, and I call in occasionally to have a coffee with her.

Neighbours were helpful for the first couple of weeks after losing Chris, but then, as is often the case, it fizzles out. I think that some people are under the impression that once the funeral is over, the bereaved person should try to bring some normality back into their lives. Following Chris's funeral, I spent the whole evening on my own. It would have been nice if I had been offered some company, especially that evening, but it wasn't to be.

In July 2018, I re-engaged in therapy as my anxiety and panic attacks had become more severe, and I was struggling to cope. At that time, I could not see a way forward. I was in a dark place, and I desperately needed help. However, yet again, I was passed from one therapist to another. I had one therapist telling me that I needed counselling for anxiety, and another one telling me that I needed bereavement counselling. Then, yet another therapist advised me that it was too soon after Chris's death to be having bereavement counselling, as it had only been a couple of months since Chris had passed away. They stated that I needed to go through the grieving process. I didn't know where I was; people were giving me conflicting information.

I started to attend weekly one-hour sessions for anxiety and panic disorder therapy. I was taken into a small room, where there were two chairs opposite each other. I was instructed where to sit. I found myself sitting directly beneath a clock which was situated on the wall above me. The therapist sat opposite me, and we started talking. She asked me numerous questions about how my anxiety impacted on my life. I also explained that I had suffered a recent bereavement. I could see that she kept glancing up at the clock, and to be honest, I felt as though I was on a meter. As soon as the hour was up, I was escorted out of the room, and a further appointment was made for the following week. Then, in went the next patient. It felt like a conveyor belt.

I gained the impression that they were striving to achieve the results that they needed in order to meet their targets. I'm in no doubt that therapy can help, and has helped numerous people in the past, and will continue to do so. However, for me, it just wasn't working. I was having sessions and coming away feeling more anxious than I did when I went in. Consequently, I stopped going. I would now concentrate on managing my anxiety myself. I would be my own therapist. I would be fine.

Christmas was approaching, yet again, and I knew that this would be the first Christmas I would be spending completely alone. I couldn't envisage how I was ever going to get through it. I hadn't celebrated Christmas properly since losing Mum in 2013; we just used to make the best of things and go with the flow. At least Chris and I were able to support each other during each festive season following Mum's death. However, this year would be a real challenge for me.

As Christmas drew closer, I received an invitation to go out for Christmas lunch. Pat, who is a close friend, and her daughter Lucy were going to a local pub for lunch and had suggested that I joined them. Lucy had been one of my bridesmaids many years ago when I married John and is every bit as lovely as her mum. It would have been the ideal invitation for me to accept, but I didn't feel that I would be able to cope with the festive atmosphere. I presumed that there would have been Christmas music playing and customers probably singing carols. It was a very emotional time of the year for me as it was my first Christmas without Chris, therefore I declined their invitation. I appreciated their concern for me over the festive period, but unfortunately on that occasion, it was probably better that I remained alone. It had been a testing time for me, and I was pleased when all the festivities were finally over. How I ever got through it, I will never know!

CHAPTER 33

Meeting Jane McDonald

Many years ago, Mum, Chris and I went to our first Jane McDonald concert at Sheffield City Hall. We had followed her on the TV documentary The Cruise but had never seen her live. Jane was a singer on The Cruise and became very popular with viewers. A couple of our friends had recently seen Jane in concert and told us how good she was and what a brilliant evening they had. I booked tickets, and we eagerly waited for the concert date to arrive. We seemed to be waiting forever, but eventually the day arrived, and we were off to the show. Jane was outstanding and the outfits she wore on stage were amazing. The sequined dresses were elegant, and she looked stunning. The audience were clapping and singing along with Jane, and it was a truly magical evening.

After the show, we managed to meet Jane and get her autograph. We waited at the stage door for a while until Jane appeared. It was lovely to chat to her; we didn't feel rushed in any way, and she was more than happy to sign the tour programme we had purchased. She chatted to us as though we were friends. She is so proud of her Yorkshire roots, just as I am, and she is so thankful to the thousands of loyal fans that support her in everything that she does. Jane is such a lovely, genuine, down-to-earth lady and one of the nicest people you could ever wish to meet. It had been a wonderful experience for us, one that we would remember - always!

We made a point of going to see Jane in concert whenever we could, visiting many different venues. One of these venues was the Royal Albert Hall in London. Everyone was on their feet, dancing and having a wonderful time. The evening was electric, and Jane was fantastic, as usual.

We always asked Jane to sign the programme at the end of the evening. She must have been shattered; she had already performed on stage for over two hours and then she would be signing autographs and chatting to fans. She became familiar with our faces, and she always gave us a hug. A Jane McDonald hug is one of the best hugs ever, and we have had many over the years.

A personally signed copy of Jane's autobiography is one of my treasured possessions. Chris and I had bought our book between us, and Mum had bought a copy too. Jane was doing a book signing in Wakefield, a city in West Yorkshire, so we went along and had our books signed. It was lovely to see her and have a chat.

Over the years, Jane has had some amazing backing singers but the one who has always stayed by Jane's side and supported her is the very lovely and talented Susan Ravey, who is a star in her own right. They have been friends for many years. Sue, like Jane, has an excellent singing voice and they complement each other.

In 2008, we went on a Jane McDonald weekend to the seaside resort of Skegness on the Lincolnshire coast, where we watched her switch on the illuminations on the Saturday and then went to see her in concert at the Embassy Theatre on the Sunday. On the Sunday afternoon, we were sitting outside a pub having a drink, and I looked towards the back of the Embassy Theatre where there was a room with a large floor-to-ceiling window. I remember saying to Mum, 'I'm sure Jane is sat in that room down there.' Mum's eyesight wasn't good so she couldn't tell whether it was Jane or not as it was some distance away from us. I said, 'Come on, we'll have a walk down.' We didn't go right up to the window, but near enough to confirm that it was Jane.

She was sitting at a table talking to an official-looking man who probably had some connection with the theatre. She spotted us and waved. We waited outside and she came out to us, gave us all a big hug, and said that it was lovely to see us. She asked if we had watched the illuminations switch-on the previous evening and I told her that we had, and that we were looking forward to the concert that evening. We had a lovely chat with her, and she said she would see us later. The evening arrived, and we were on a high as we were on our way to see Jane. The concert was fantastic, and we had an excellent time. She has written and performed some beautiful songs which have reduced many audiences to tears, including us.

When Jane is on stage, she is so funny. We have always said that if she ever stopped singing, she would make a good comedienne. She makes off-the-cuff remarks and has been known to have a joke with Susan

Ravey. She is very witty and knows exactly how to interact with her audience, and always manages to get everyone on their feet by the end of the evening.

Throughout the years, we have always enjoyed collecting memorabilia and have amassed some lovely photos and posters of Jane. At various shows, I can recall fans taking posters from the walls in order to keep them as souvenirs, although at some venues the management weren't too happy and didn't allow it. They should have done what I did and asked first if they could have a poster, instead of just removing them from the wall, which is something I would never have done. Before each show we went to, I always rang the venue and asked if they would kindly save me a poster to be collected at the end of the evening, and the majority were always obliging. It just goes to show, if you go about things in the correct way, you often get the result that you are looking for.

Just before Mum's seventieth birthday, I wrote to Jane and asked her if she would send Mum a signed photograph, and she was more than happy to do so. The photograph arrived, and Mum was over the moon to see that Jane had written a birthday message and signed it. She placed it in a frame and hung it on the wall.

We have followed Jane for many years but unfortunately, I was unable to attend any of Jane's concerts in the years after the loss of my mum. We were so close, and I would have found it too distressing to go to one of Jane's concerts without Mum and Chris. At every concert Jane used to sing 'You're My World,' which she dedicates to her fans, and as Jane used to start singing the song, Mum would always take hold of my hand and give it a gentle squeeze. Then the tissues used to come out. That was the last song I had played at Mum's funeral as it was what Mum had requested. As you can imagine, it has immense significance to me. As far as I was aware, Jane still sang this song at her concerts, and I didn't want to go because I knew I would find it too difficult to sit and listen to. Sorry, Jane! It was still early days for me. I know that Jane will be reading this, as she has requested a copy.

After writing the first draft of this chapter, I decided to book tickets to see Jane live on 3rd September 2021. I knew it would be an emotional evening for me, as it was going to bring back such a lot of memories, but it is something that I was looking forward to.

The evening at Sheffield City Hall was amazing. My friend and I made our way to our seats, and eagerly awaited Jane's appearance on stage. The lights went down, the music started playing, and Jane walked on stage. She was met with huge applause as her fans clapped and cheered. My eyes welled up; I had waited years for this moment. She looked stunning. During the evening, Jane wore some amazing outfits. It was a wonderful evening, and Jane sang some beautiful, emotional songs, which brought many in the audience to tears - including myself!

Message to Jane:

Thank you so much for being a part of our lives and providing us with excellent entertainment for over twenty years. You are a wonderful, talented lady, and it has been a privilege to be able to follow your journey.

Keep doing what you do - nobody does it better!

Thank you so much, Jane and Sue, for entertaining your loyal fans, not only at your latest concert, but over many years.

CHAPTER 34

Reminiscing About Mum

C hris and I used to spend most evenings at Mum's, putting the world to rights, as you do. I used to love listening to Mum's endless stories about what life was like when she was growing up. I have always found older people interesting and feel that when an older person dies, a library is lost. Mum was born in 1939 and always stated that she was a war baby. She told stories of hearing the sirens, and the family having to make their way to the air raid shelter.

Mum was an accomplished pianist in her younger days. She related how she would play music in the evening on the piano, which took pride of place in the living room. She passed numerous music and piano playing exams leading up to one final exam, which would have qualified her to teach piano if she had passed it. However, she didn't sit that exam and ended up giving up piano playing altogether. She told me that she was sick of studying and longed to spend time with her friends, doing all the things that people her age were doing. She always supposed that it must have been a great disappointment to her parents.

She described her strict upbringing. As she got

older, she used to go out dancing in the evening but always had to be back home by 10 pm. That was the cut-off point of her evening. Apparently, in those days, if you were out too late, you were up to no good. I don't know what they thought you would be doing after 10 pm that you couldn't have done before 10 pm. However, that was the rule, and she had to abide by it. This curfew was in place right up until she was twenty-one years of age, which was when you got the key to the door, and you finally became an adult.

Mum also had a beautiful singing voice and used to perform in some of the clubs in our local area. However, after she married, she didn't continue with her singing, as my father wouldn't allow her to. I loved to hear her singing around the house, she had a lovely voice, and I was so proud of her.

We enjoyed going shopping together and often used to have lunch out, which Mum would pay for as a way of saying thank you for taking her to town. She always said that if it wasn't for me, she wouldn't get into town as she would never feel comfortable going on her own because of health issues. This of course didn't always sit well with me because I was never comfortable with her paying for lunch each time. However, I always got my own back by treating her to some of her favourite chocolates. I loved treating her; she was very special to me. I adored making a fuss of her and making her feel special, which is exactly what she was - always!

I could never understand why some mothers and daughters didn't see eye to eye and would argue and fall out on a regular basis. This is something that we never did! Yes, we used to have a difference of opinion, once in a while, but we never argued, and we certainly never ever fell out with each other. She was my world, and I could never have imagined a day when we didn't speak - it wouldn't have happened. I am unable to comprehend why anyone would want to fall out with their own mother. I adored her and always tried to make sure that she was the happiest that I could possibly make her.

She was an emotional person and easily became upset about things, more so as she got older, so I always tried to ensure that her life was stress-free. I would organise appointments for her and fill in any forms that needed filling in. I took care of her 'life admin.'

I have many fond memories of holidays in Scarborough with Mum and Chris. On the day we were setting off, Mum was always so excited, like a little kid going on holiday for the first time. I loved seeing her so excited - her sense of anticipation was infectious, so I always knew that we were going to have a lovely holiday. We used to stay in a four-star ground floor apartment up in the old town, close to the market. We loved Scarborough and particularly enjoyed sitting and looking out to sea. There is something very calming and relaxing about water, you can almost lose yourself as you watch the waves ebb and flow. I could watch it for hours. I always made a point of treating Mum to something nice while we were on holiday. As she was fond of chocolate, I would often take her to a posh chocolate shop to choose something special while we were there. Mum was partial to milk or dark chocolate, coffee creams in particular. She would always choose a varied selection.

We had many holidays together in various parts

of the country, ranging from the southwest up to the northeast of England and areas in between. We went down to Looe many years ago and toured the numerous different parts of Cornwall, taking in the beauty of the many picturesque towns and villages. A favourite of ours was the charming village of Polperro, with its narrow winding streets and lanes, and great views of the picturesque harbour. Everything about Cornwall is beautiful, and we loved it there. Unfortunately, it was such a long journey to get there, and Chris was the only driver, so we didn't go often.

I will always remember coming home after the first holiday in Cornwall. We had been sampling the Cornish fare while we were there and decided to take various items home with us. By the time we had finished, you would have thought that we had done a weekly shop at the supermarket. We brought pasties home with us, which were absolutely delicious. You've not had a pasty until you've had a proper Cornish pasty, eaten in Cornwall. We also brought some fresh crab, Cornish butter, cheese, bread, and Cornish ice cream. We had a large cool box and a cool bag which we packed everything into, surrounded by ice blocks and bags of ice cubes. Strangely enough, nothing tasted as nice when eating it at home as it had done in Cornwall. We wondered why this is often the case.

We also went touring in the Lake District, taking in the beautiful views of Lakeland. We stayed in Ambleside, and made trips to Keswick, Coniston, Windermere, and Grasmere. All the lakes were picturesque although my personal favourite was Lake Windermere. The rugged scenery of hills and mountains surrounding the lake was breath-taking.

We had some lovely meals in the Lake District, although some of them were quite expensive at that time. We went to a pub for lunch in Ambleside one day and just ordered sandwiches as we didn't want a full meal. Our food arrived, and we had never seen anything like it. The waiter put a plate of sandwiches with a few crisps and salad garnish in front of each of us. All I can say is that I would have loved to have seen the size of the loaf that the crusty white bread was cut from; it must have been a foot high! The sandwiches were enormous, and the bread was the freshest, tastiest bread we had ever eaten. The sandwiches were packed full of our choice of filling, and there was no way we were ever going to eat all that was in front of us. We took some back to where we were staying to eat later. We had some lovely holidays and made some great memories to look back on.

Mum and I both had a good sense of humour and were always laughing about something. We both knew just how to make each other laugh. I'm witty, therefore I was always saying something funny. Both Mum and Chris always expressed that I would have made a good comedienne if I had been confident enough to go on stage. Sadly, I wasn't. It's one thing to come out with a few funny one-liners to make people laugh, but to stand on stage for two hours and cause the audience to cry tears of laughter takes some doing, and I admire anyone who can do that.

Mum and I would laugh at anything and everything, and sometimes we were guilty of laughing at things we shouldn't have. Sometimes we would be in someone's company, and they would say something that we found amusing. They couldn't see the funny side of what they had said, but Mum and I did. We could not look at each other because if we had, we would have cracked out laughing. Chris often used to say that I had a weird sense of humour. She had a good sense of humour, but not the same as the sense of humour Mum and I shared.

Mum wasn't very tall; she was only four feet eleven inches later in life. She used to be five feet but as everyone knows, you do shrink a little as you get older. However, when you are only five feet to start off with, you can't afford to shrink. Of course, she had to endure all the jokes that come with being small. I would often make jokes about her being short. I used to say to her, 'I wouldn't say you are small, mother, but when it rains, you are the last one to get wet. There are gnomes that get wet before you do.'

She would say, 'I'm going to hit you in a minute.'

I would say, 'And who's going to lift you up to do that?'

It was all said in fun, and she always took it well. I always knew how far to go, and I would never have upset her for the world. In fact, we all used to laugh at each other regarding something or other. If you give it out, you have to be prepared to take it.

Anyone who knew us often commented on how close we were. I was once telling a friend how much I miss Mum and how I didn't feel that I would ever come to terms with losing her, and she said, 'You were inseparable.'

Recently, while out with one of my friends, we were talking about Mum and reminiscing about some of the good laughs we had shared with her. My friend said, 'I loved your mum.' I was touched. Mum always got on well with my friends. She liked them all, and they all liked Mum.

Mum was the nicest, kindest person that you could ever wish to meet. She didn't judge people, and always accepted them for who they were. She always supported Chris and I with our relationship from day one. She was always happy to offer help if people needed it, and often put the needs of others before her own. I was devastated beyond words when Mum passed away. She had been both mother and father to me. She was my beautiful mum, my mentor, and my best friend, and I was so proud to call her my mum. I will keep my memories of her safely tucked away in my heart - always.

AND FINALLY ...

Thank you for taking the time to read my book! I wouldn't normally be so open with people as I prefer to keep things private. However, this is a book that needed to be written, and I knew that, one day, everything I wanted to say would be documented and published. I have surprised myself with the amount of information that I have shared within my book.

The eagle-eyed will notice that there are certain pieces of information that I haven't included in this book - I'm sure they will talk about this amongst themselves. I feel that I have disclosed quite a lot about my life in this book. There are aspects that I haven't included as they will always remain private between me, Mum and Chris. Not every ounce of your life needs to be documented.

Writing this book has been one of the hardest things I have ever done. Part-way through writing, along with other health problems, I was diagnosed with fibromyalgia. Therefore, I suffer with widespread pain, extreme fatigue, and problems with attention and concentration, also known as fibro-fog. However, I was at the point of no return, and felt that I had to continue writing as I was determined to publish my memoir.

It was more difficult than I had initially thought.

It has opened up so many old wounds and brought back a plethora of emotions. The first chapter was one of the hardest chapters for me to write, as it reminded me of a childhood that was taken away from me. When I had completed the chapter, I sat back while it was read out to me and sobbed. It really hit home - what life had been like for Mum and me until we made the break away from my father.

Chris and I had many conversations about my childhood and how my father had treated me. She once asked me how I would feel if I ever found out that he had passed away. I told her that his passing wouldn't affect me in any way. She wondered if it would affect me more than I initially thought, as I would be wishing that things could have been different between us. Quite a few years ago, Mum and I bumped into one of my cousins in town, and she informed us that my father had passed away. I felt nothing whatsoever. There was no sadness, no tears, in fact, it was as though she had told me that a stranger had died. I hated the man, for what he put me and Mum through. I certainly wasn't going to shed any tears over him.

Mum was the special parent in my life. She was the one who was always there for me, often going without to provide for me. She was a very special lady, and she meant the world to me.

It was difficult for me to write about my relationship with Chris. As you are aware, I started right at the beginning, when Chris and I first met. Our first kiss, our first night together, and everything that followed in our relationship. I was okay while I was actually writing, as it felt as though I was reliving the time Chris and I were together. While I was writing about her, it was as though she was there with me. It felt as if everything that I was writing was happening at that moment, but sadly, it wasn't. Then, I would finish writing, shut down my laptop, and reality would kick in. I would go to pieces and start having panic attacks because I know that I will never see her again. I'm finding it so hard, as writing this book has made me fall madly in love with her, all over again. It also deeply saddens me that we weren't together when she passed away.

Since losing Mum and Chris, my anxiety and panic attacks are the worst that they have ever been. I am often woken up in the middle of the night because of a panic attack. My heart will be pounding, I will be shaking, and all I want right at that moment is for Chris to be there with me. I feel that I need to put my arms around her and hold her so close to me. It's a terrible feeling, and frightening. I will never come to terms with losing Mum and Chris.

People are under the impression that I'm doing okay, because that's how I portray myself in public. They will ask how I'm doing because it's the polite thing to do. I usually tell them that I'm doing fine. It's easier to say that than start telling people how I'm really feeling. Very often, they want to hear that a person is doing okay. If you start to tell them anything different, they often feel uncomfortable, and suddenly haven't got time to sit and listen. It's so much easier to say, 'I'm fine.' The truth is, I have never felt so alone, and miserable in all my life. However, I go out, I put a smile on my face, and no one would ever know anything different.

People don't fake being depressed; they fake being

happy, for the benefit of others. It's easy to go out with friends, have a laugh, and crack a few jokes. Then, when the evening is over, it's just as easy to go back home and break down again. That's the side that people don't see. I have friends who have been marvellous since I lost Chris - they know who they are. I also have friends who have sat back and watched me struggle because they are often too busy when I need to talk - they also know who they are.

As you will have already read, at the beginning of this book, my best friend, when I first started working, was Jean. We were very close, did lots of things together, and went out on a regular basis. She would also stay at the flat sometimes, with me and Mum. Consequently, I was questioned about our relationship on a number of occasions by a member of staff who we worked with. She held a higher position than Jean and I. She, and other members of staff, were under the impression that Jean and I were having a relationship. I confirmed that we weren't. However, she went on to question me on further occasions. Apparently, according to her, some of the girls we worked with had strong suspicions that Jean and I were together. She would never tell me the names of the people who suspected this. All she would say is that people were talking.

For anyone out there, who let their imagination go into overdrive many years ago, I'm going to take the opportunity to set the record straight about the relationship I had, and continue to have, with one of my closest friends. There was never, there isn't now, and there never will be anything other than friendship between me and Jean. She is one of my closest friends, and

I love her to bits, but only as a friend. I'm not, and never have been, in love with her. She is happily married, with a beautiful family, and is most definitely not gay. She is aware of my feelings of friendship towards her, and she is also aware that I am writing this and setting the record straight. It's a pity that people had nothing better to do than make assumptions about close friends.

Would I change anything about my life? The answer to that question is, 'Yes.' If I could, I would change around 75% of the things that have happened in my life. One thing I definitely wouldn't change is my relationship with Chris, and the time we spent together. Those were the happiest days of my life, and I know that they were the happiest days of Chris's life too. There was nothing that we wouldn't do for each other. We were so protective of each other. She was my world; we were devoted, and I'm still so in love with her.

I get on fine with men as friends, but I could never enter into another relationship with a man. Living with an abusive father, and the problems I encountered within my marriage, did a lot of damage. I know there are some wonderful men out there who are role models for husbands and fathers, and how things should be within a relationship. However, I'm gay, and men just don't do it for me.

Would I recommend going down the road of a gay relationship? That depends on several factors. If a gay person asked my advice on whether to start a gay relationship, my advice would be this: 'Don't rush into anything.'

Once you enter into a gay relationship, your life changes in ways you could never have imagined. You will encounter many disapproving glares because you are in a same-sex relationship. You could lose friends or even family members as not everyone will be accepting of your relationship. You will encounter verbal abuse from homophobic people. These are things that you might have to deal with on a daily basis. You need to be certain that being in a gay relationship is the path you want to go down. If you're not 100% certain, I would advise that you take as much time as you need to think about the journey you will be making, because it is going to have an effect on your whole life. You will know in your heart of hearts if you are destined for a life with a same-sex partner.

Chris and I made a point of not broadcasting our relationship. However, it's surprising how many people seemed to know. I bet that news travelled faster than a greyhound out of a trap.

Chris and I were meant to be together. She was my first, and one and only, love. I had no problem walking away from my marriage, but Chris and I could never have walked away from each other. It wasn't always hearts and flowers; we argued from time to time, as do most people in any relationship. To be honest, the majority of our arguments were due to opinionated people claiming that what we were doing was wrong. We were besotted with each other, and nobody could have come between us. We lived together for thirty-two years - not bad, especially as we were told right at the beginning that our relationship would be a flash in the pan!

Chris and I got together in the 1980s. It was a different world then, and I was unsure how to deal with my sexuality. Society is more accepting of same-sex relationships now, in the way that gay marriage is permitted. We have come a long way; gay relationships aren't frowned upon as much as they once were. However, we still have a long way to go. I don't feel that lesbians and gay men will ever be fully accepted in society - certainly not in my lifetime.

People may try to discourage you from travelling down that road, but you have to stay true to yourself, and not allow others to plan your life. If you are 100% certain that sharing your life with a same-sex partner is what you want, then my advice would be, 'Go for it.' However, you will both need to be strong to survive in a world that still isn't fully accepting of same-sex relationships. If it's meant to be, no one will keep you apart. Stay strong, be there for each other, and together, you will overcome everything that life throws at you - just as we did!

While writing this book, I was asked if I would be including any sex scenes. The person who asked the question looked so disappointed when I told them that I wouldn't, for which I make no apologies. Yes, I have made reference to Chris and I sleeping together, as we both agreed on this when Chris was alive. There was no way I intended breaching that agreement. I'm a firm believer in what happens between a couple in the bedroom should stay in the bedroom. Whatever you and your partner choose to do when you are in bed, leave it at the bedroom door on your way out. There is no need to share that with other people. It's called having respect for your partner.

The friends I currently have in my life are the people I want in my life. There were people who Mum and Chris were confident that I would be able to rely on once they had passed away and I was on my own. However, since losing Chris, some of these people have turned their backs and walked away. Initially, I missed not having those people in my life, but as the saying goes, it is what it is. Now, I could never accept those people back into my life. I thought they were friends, but they turned and walked away at a time when I was at my absolute lowest. As far as I'm concerned, they can keep on walking. This signifies one thing - they were never true friends!

I'm wary of people. I tend to study a person when I meet them. I'm not that trusting, especially when a person's actions don't match their words. I feel that this stems from being let down on so many occasions since losing Mum and Chris, with people making promises, and not delivering. I would never trust someone who tells you other people's secrets. If I am told something in confidence, I never share that information with anyone. Unless I am told otherwise, I would take it to the grave.

I continue to live my life with anxiety and many phobias. I can't predict the future, but I'm optimistic and believe that one day things will change. The past few years have been the worst years of my life, and I've had to be strong in order to survive. You can't put a time limit on grieving. You never stop grieving - you just learn how to cope with it, because you have no choice. However, life does go on and I am fortunate enough to have some wonderful friends who I know will always be there for me.

I have lost the two most important people in my life, which is something that I will never come to terms with. Mum and Chris were my world, and I always knew that their passing would have a damaging effect on my health. I'm not the same person as I was when Mum and Chris were alive. I'm a lot more emotional than I used to be. I can laugh about something one minute, then a minute later, I'm in floods of tears. I always said that I would struggle to cope without Mum and Chris, but I could never have imagined that it would hit me so hard. I'm broken without them. I'm trying so hard to rebuild my life but finding it so difficult. I feel as though I'm climbing a mountain, and as soon as I get so far up, there is someone waiting to knock me back down. I feel that with the right level of support, and more company, I would be a lot further forward. But sadly, some people just haven't got the time! It also depends where you feature on their list of priorities.

It would also appear that the art of conversation is rapidly dying. Nowadays, people would rather spend time writing a text message than actually speaking. My thoughts on this are as follows:

'If you've got time to write a text message, you've got time to press a button on your phone to call someone. Try it more often - exercise your vocal cords! You never know, it could make someone's day.'

When Mum and Chris were alive, I felt safe. I felt as though I had a purpose in life. Falling in love with Chris changed my life, and living without her has done the same. I'm not the same person as I was when she was alive. When Mum and Chris passed away, part of me went with them. Everything has changed, and I need to rebuild my life and try to regain some form of normality. I'm not yet where I want to be, but I'm a long way from where I was. For now, I'm the best that I can be!

Own up to your mistakes. Apologise when you're wrong, and never take anything for granted. Everything could change in the blink of an eye - and for me, it did!

Why did I choose *Defying the Odds* as the title for this book? There were three main reasons:

My father always claimed that Mum and I would never make it on our own.

My ex-husband stated that Chris and I wouldn't last, and that he would destroy us.

Chris's sister claimed that our relationship would be a flash in the pan.

If anyone reading this book is in an abusive relationship, please be aware that there is help out there. When there are more tears than laughter, and more pain than happiness, it's time to walk away. This is what Mum and I did, and we never looked back. Then, years later, I walked away from my marriage. From a young age, I vowed that I would never stay in a relationship with a partner who was controlling. Remember you are only ever one decision away from a completely different life. If reading my book has helped just one person - my work is done!

From the word go, the odds were stacked against us. Many people thought that we would fail, on all levels. However, we remained strong, and we succeeded. I'm proud to say that we most certainly *Defied the Odds.*

MY WORLD
WITHOUT MUM

My world has been torn apart,
My life is now a darker place,
For I have felt lost and lonely,
Broken, emptiness, a sad face.

Once you were here, by my side,
Full of laughter, love and grace,
But now as I look beside me,
I see nothing but an empty space.

I think of you and reminisce,
But still I hurt so much inside,
I'm looking for the answers,
Searching for the reason why.

Each day I live, I wipe the tears,
That gently fall upon my face,
Longing to have you near me,
To be together one more day.

I cannot come to terms with it,
My life will never be the same,
How do I survive without you?
Trying to face each new day.

The love I have inside for you,
Could never ever be denied,
If my love could've saved you,
You never would have died.

Holding onto precious memories,
That we once shared together,
Staying locked within my heart,
Where you will always be, forever.

I know you're watching over me,
As I look at the stars up in the sky,
And will help me through this pain,
Guiding me as each day goes by.

The bond we shared was special,
Which was always plain to see,
And you will always keep me safe,
Best friends forever, you and me.

God bless my precious mum
For never will there be
A mum who is as special
As what you are to me.

I Love You.

FOR THE ONE
I LOVE

You came into my life and took my hand,
we walked through a field of emotions on
our journey to a promised land. Our hands
locked, together we were climbing on the
ladder that took us to the stars. Your kiss
was soft like gentle rain, tenderly falling
upon my lips. You held me close and you
loved me, you taught me how to live again.
I will always keep our special memories
safely tucked away within my heart. I
cherished every moment spent with you,
your loving smile, your gentle touch, the
words you spoke that meant so much.
I miss you so, now that you're gone, though
our love will always be eternal, two hearts
entwined that shall forever remain as one.

I Love You.

YORKSHIRE

It's not all flat caps and whippets *tha* knows,
It's Yorkshire puddings with lashings of gravy.
It's pie *un* peas, *un* fish and chips on a tray,
Always eaten in newspaper back in the day.
In steamy vinegar'd paper, how good they tasted,
A real treat, all eaten up, not a morsel wasted.

It's the St Leger, betting on a horse, watchin' it run,
Hoping it's not a donkey and you've got a good *'un*.
By 'eck it's grand this county with all its dales,
And sheep takin' priority on our country lanes.
Roaming to pastures new, not a care as they go,
And always making drivers wait, and rightly so!

The gruelling industry of steel and coal,
Men working underground in a black hole.
Soot marked faces, and worn out hands,
Lost daylight hours as they mined our land.
The Flying Scotsman, Mallard, trains of steam,
Pleasing to the eye as their colours gleam.

It's *'ows tha doin'*? *C'mon in and take a pew,*
Putting the world to rights, over a welcome brew,
That liquid gold destined to light up any face,
Always an empty mug, never leaving a trace,
It's Yorkshire, the White Rose, God's own county,
Green and pleasant, *my favourite chuffin' place.*

ACKNOWLEDGEMENTS

A big thank you to my special mum, the one who was always there for me with unconditional love. I miss you more than words could ever say. Always in my thoughts, forever in my heart.

Thank you to my partner, my first love, for the wonderful years that we spent together. I miss you so much. Our love is eternal.

For always being there, encouraging me, and helping to make my dream come true, I'm eternally grateful to you both. This always kept me focussed while writing my book.

Special thanks to my editor, Roz Andrews, for her time, patience, encouragement, and invaluable advice. Roz has done an excellent job, and the quality of her work has been outstanding. Her knowledge, efficiency, and correspondence have been second to none, and it has been an absolute pleasure to work with her.

Thanks to graphic designer Laura Leonard for designing my book cover. I appreciate your patience while I was choosing my preferred design. It was a pleasure to work with you.

Thanks to marketing coach Teju Chosen for your help and advice.

Thanks to author Clarice Jane for designing and producing my promotional video and book trailer, and for providing advice while writing this book.

For special friends who have helped me through a difficult time in my life, thank you for your support and praise while writing this book. For the times that we spend together, and the memories that we share, thank you - I cherish your friendship.

Many thanks to Jane McDonald and Susan Ravey for allowing me to include you in one of my chapters.

Last but not least, thank you to everyone who has supported me on my journey while writing this book - your support, advice and encouragement are truly appreciated!

ABOUT THE AUTHOR

Pauline Thompson

Pauline Thompson was born in South Yorkshire in 1961. At school she was affectionately known as the class clown and would frequently amuse her fellow classmates and teachers with her witty banter.

Even as a teenager, she enjoyed writing and kept a diary. She always felt that a diary would be interesting to look back on, many years later. As a young adult, she took a break from writing to concentrate on other aspects of her life. However, that was short-lived as she was missing the therapy of documenting her day-to-day life. She was optimistic that one day she would write and publish a book about her life, and without these diaries, this wouldn't have been possible.

Over the past few years, Pauline has picked up her pen once again and published her debut poetry collection Say What You Feel in 2020. Poems from that book have been featured on BBC Radio Sheffield.

This book has been incredibly difficult to write as it has brought back a plethora of emotions. However, Pauline felt that now was the right time to put pen to paper and write her story. She has worked with some amazing people on the journey to having this book published and has learned a lot.

BOOKS BY THIS AUTHOR

Say What You Feel

Heartfelt poetry portraying life as I now live it following the loss of the two special people in my life. This book touches on things close to my heart and depicts the world we live in today, and memories of years gone by.

This is my debut collection of forty poems which will take you from tears to laughter at the turn of a page. You will find it witty, emotional and nostalgic.

This book will resonate with many readers who have suffered loss and continue to fight the battle of acceptance. Once you start reading it will take you on a journey where you will want to travel until you reach the end.

Printed in Great Britain
by Amazon